This book belongs to:

_____

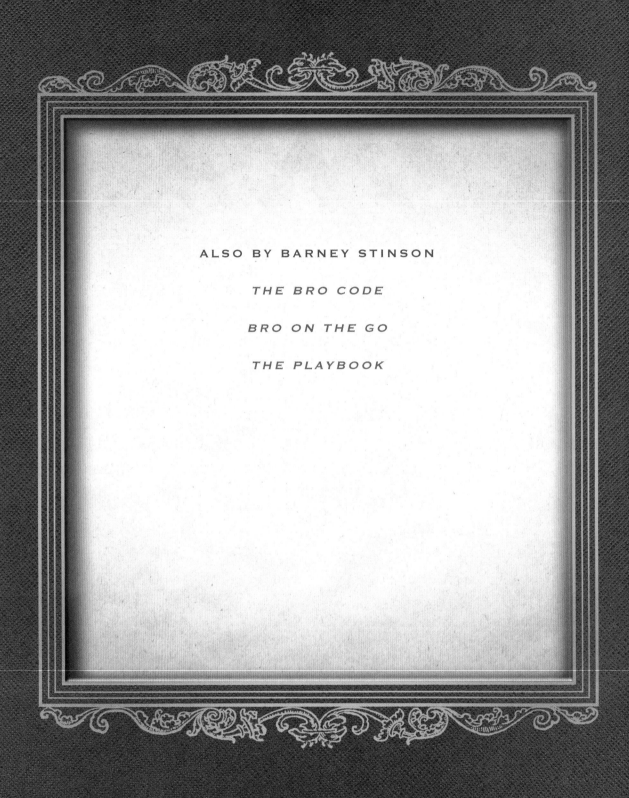

ALSO BY BARNEY STINSON

THE BRO CODE

BRO ON THE GO

THE PLAYBOOK

THE BRO CODE FOR PARENTS

WHAT TO EXPECT WHEN YOU'RE AWESOME

Barney Stinson

with MATT KUHN

A TOUCHSTONE BOOK
PUBLISHED BY SIMON & SCHUSTER

NEW YORK   LONDON   TORONTO   SYDNEY   NEW DELHI

Touchstone
A Division of Simon & Schuster, Inc.
1230 Avenue of the Americas
New York, NY 10020

First Touchstone trade paperback edition October 2012

TOUCHSTONE and colophon are registered trademarks of Simon & Schuster, Inc.

For information about special discounts for bulk purchases, please contact Simon & Schuster Special Sales at 1-866-506-1949 or business@simonandschuster.com.

The Simon & Schuster Speakers Bureau can bring authors to your live event. For more information or to book an event contact the Simon & Schuster Speakers Bureau at 1-866-248-3049 or visit our website at www.simonspeakers.com.

Designed by Ruth Lee-Mui
Illustrations by Tom Richmond

Manufactured in the United States of America

1   3   5   7   9   10   8   6   4   2

Library of Congress Cataloging-in-Publication Data
Stinson, Barney.
The bro code for parents : what to expect when you're awesome /
Barney Stinson ; with Matt Kuhn. — 1st Touchstone trade paperback ed.
    p.   cm.
1. Pregnancy—Humor.   2. Motherhood—Humor.
3. Fatherhood—Humor.   I. Kuhn, Matt.   II. Title.
PN6231.P68S75 2012
808.87—dc23   2012020894

ISBN 978-1-4516-9058-3
ISBN 978-1-4516-9064-4 (ebook)

For Marvin Waitforit Eriksen . . .

*May this book help you lead the awesome life your parents,
Marshall and Lily, can never give you*

DISCLAIMER

Despite what I may have suggested to countless hotties, I am not, nor ever have been, a licensed pediatrician, psychologist, or international spy. As such, the opinions, techniques, and alarmingly comprehensive parenting advice presented throughout this gospel should never be construed as commonly accepted fact or scientifically proven medical truth, even when expressly presented as such. Except for the section on infant CPR . . . that's pretty much spot-on.

Note: The parodies of real books included in *The Bro Code for Parents* are not affiliated with the actual books in any way, and were not done with the permission of their publishers or authors . . . which should be pretty obvious, because mine are far more awesome.

CONTENTS

INTRODUCTION

Congratulations! If you're reading this very important book, then you've made the momentous decision to cannonball headfirst into the waterless pool of parenthood. Your world is about to fundamentally and permanently change in ways you could never have anticipated. You're excited, overwhelmed, and probably a little scared at the prospect of raising a child and no doubt riddled with serious concerns about your future:

- Will I be a good parent?
- Can I afford to give my child the life she deserves?
- Will I ever have pleasurable sex again?
- After I squeeze this kid out of my uterus, will I ever regain my slamming hot bod?
- Can I really ever love this child as much as I love my own life?

Rest at ease because the answer to all of these questions is a rock-solid no. Your life is over, Bro. *Done.* Curtains. Guess what? We all took a vote and you're the new mayor of Loserville. I mean . . . obviously I didn't vote, because I'm not a loser. But you know who is? You. A big, fat, dumb one.

But there is hope. Just because your existence is suddenly a petrifying turd on the canvas of life doesn't mean your kid has to be the insecure, socially inept, unhygienic basket case you're about to become. And that's why I've written this book—to help you raise an awesome, kickass kid who will live the legendary life you no longer can because of the emotionally and financially crippling decision you just made. But seriously, thanks for buying the book.

WHY I WROTE THIS AWESOME BOOK

You might be wondering why I, Barney "the Cooter King" Stinson, have written a book about pregnancy and parenthood when I'm not a father and have, in fact, spent the lion's share of my adult life cunningly avoiding exactly this type of life-destroying affliction. The answer is simple: money, bitches! Just kidding. I also wrote it because when my good friends Marshall and Lily gave birth to their first child, I realized that without me he'd never learn important lifelong skills like "setting insects on fire" or "learning to go upskirt" or "strategic boner concealment."

And why do I want to help others? Because I *care*.

- I care about the countless young parents who senselessly sacrifice their lives only to raise kids who believe soccer is a legitimate sport.
- I care about the millions of children who are taught "sharing" and "listening" instead of real-world skills like "lying" and "using people to get what you want."
- And most important, I care about America.

That's right, when people think of Barney Stinson, they immediately think of one thing: "giant multiorgasmic penis." The next thing they think is "God-fearing patriot . . . who happens to have a giant multiorgasmic penis." You see, I believe that the next generation of Americans can overcome the many shortcomings of their lame parents and one day be as awesome as I am. Then we will be not only the greatest nation on the planet, but also the best dressed.*

---

* Note to foreign readers: Please don't be offended by my patriotism. If there's one thing we've all learned over the last decade it's that everyone the world over loves America . . . and whether you like it or not, that includes you.

In short, I'm writing this book because the so-called parenting experts have been leading our children down the wrong path. And I'm not at all writing this book because my friends Marshall and Lily just had a baby and I'm terrified that I won't be important to them anymore unless it seems like I know lots of cool stuff about babies . . . so I don't see why you're even suggesting that.

ABOUT THIS AWESOME BOOK

I've organized *The Bro Code for Parents* in a chronological fashion that will guide you from getting a baby in someone's stomach, to getting the baby out of said stomach, to finally dumping the baby off at preschool . . . basically the entire scope of parenting.

Interspersed throughout the book are a number of stories, songs, and exercises aimed at injecting some fun into the learning process. For example, would you rather sit your child down and lecture him on the differences between boys and girls or impart this crucial lesson through the illustrated nursery rhyme "Little Bo Peep Show"? Feel free to skip ahead to those interludes at any point because it's important to teach your child as soon as possible that reading suuuuuuuucks!

Lastly, try to have fun with the process. Parenting should be the most rewarding endeavor you ever undertake. Personally I don't buy it, but you hear it all the time, so it must be true.

If after reading this comprehensive and informative guide you still find yourself a little lost as a parent, just remember, at the end of the day, the goal is pretty simple:

Raise a daughter who doesn't grow up to be a stripper and
a son who grows up to bang one.

Good luck.

PART I

HOW TO GET PREGNANT

❧

If you are reading this book, you're either pregnant or desperately want to be. If you are already expecting a child, congratulations! Feel free to skip ahead to the next section or at the very least past this next paragraph.

If you're not pregnant, this is your last chance to avoid what could be the biggest mistake you'll ever make. Children are loud, expensive, smelly, and expensive. Worse, even if you're hell-bent on having one, it can be harder than you think to produce a drooling anchor of flesh that promises to weigh you down until the day you die and more than likely long, long after.

Perhaps your parents or a well-meaning teacher led you to believe that you can get pregnant simply by having sex. As I've explained to countless young women in private seminars all over the world, that is simply not true . . . provided you don't talk, face each other, or ever communicate again.

The truth of the matter is that the road to pregnancy can be an arduous, painful, and emotional journey. You might spend several years and thousands of dollars with nothing more to show for the effort than a slight limp and some curious bruises from all the kinky bedroom stuff you hopefully got to try.

So before you take your first steps toward guaranteed depression of one form or another, it's important to prepare yourself for everything that trying to get pregnant entails.

ARE YOU READY TO BE A PARENT?

As you consider having a child, one of the first questions you should ask yourself is, "Am I sober right now?" We've all made a poor decision while drunk, be it reenacting the van surfing scene from *Teen Wolf* or sleeping with a balding chick or commandeering a police horse to escape the balding chick . . . but this is too important a decision to make while under the influence of alcohol.

The question you really need to ask yourself is, "Am I ready to be a parent?" Becoming a mother or a father requires a whole new set of responsibilities, such as

- Getting home every single night before 3 AM
- Trading in your wardrobe for ugly sweaters and high-riding "slacks"
- Watching and having an informed opinion on each week's *Extreme Makeover: Home Edition*
- Paying taxes
- Having sex almost exclusively with just one other person

Many people are understandably nervous about these types of lifestyle changes and aren't ready to trade in an invigorating social life, geographic mobility, disposable income, a rewarding sense of self, relative quiet, exercise, a flexible calendar, and regular sleep patterns for the joy of wiping diarrhea off a baby's legs, hands, and face.

To help answer whether you're really ready for parenthood, try filling out the following lifestyle quiz.

LIFESTYLE QUIZ

On a scale of 1 to 5, with 1 being "a few hours" and 5 being "every waking moment," how much of your day is spent engaged in the following activities?

ACTIVITY	A FEW HOURS		EVERY WAKING MOMENT		
laser tag	1	2	3	4	5
porn	1	2	3	4	5
video gaming	1	2	3	4	5
trash-talking Bros about video gaming	1	2	3	4	5
drinking	1	2	3	4	5
managing your financial investments	1	2	3	4	5
managing your fantasy sports teams	1	2	3	4	5
thinking up imaginative "who would win in a fight between" scenarios	1	2	3	4	5
throwing things out of windows	1	2	3	4	5
being awesome	1	2	3	4	5

Total up your answers to learn your Lifestyle Score and then refer to the answer key below.

LIFESTYLE SCORE

10–25 **Sad Sack**—A baby will not seriously interrupt your pathetically lame life. Go ahead and crank one out!

26–40 **No-Man's-Land**—It's time to either commit to a fulfilling life of rewarding challenges or just give up and have a child.

41–50 **Legendary**—You are living the dream. Do you really want to throw it all away on some kid you don't even know?

ARE YOU FINANCIALLY READY?

Another important factor as you consider parenthood is your financial picture. Even the cheapest babies will run you as much as twenty dollars a month, which to put it in perspective, is roughly the cost of *two* premium cable channels . . . and I don't know if you've been watching, but Showtime's really picked up its game.

As is so often the case when making an important decision, it helps to stop for a moment and look at things on paper. And after you've paid a little visit to your printed porn collection, you might want to consider creating a baby budget.

Below is a chart depicting some of the financial considerations a responsible parent might make in a typical month.

TYPICAL MONTHLY BABY BUDGET
(in US dollars . . . duh)

CATEGORY	COST
BABY FOOD	
Honey Smacks (72 single-serve boxes)	$160.00
Mountain Dew (10 cases)	$190.00
ramen noodle (pack of 24)	$5.52
MEDICAL EXPENSES	
Alka-Seltzer	$13.22
Band-Aids	$7.99

WARDROBE	
disposable onesies	$350.00
replacing your spit-upon designer suits/outfits	$12,500.00
diapers	$0.00
	(Burger King napkins don't cost a dime)

TOYS	
old tennis ball	$0.00
plastic bag	$0.00
450cc 4x4 Sport ATV	$6,999.00

ENTERTAINMENT	
The Wire box set	$150.00
plastic bag	See above.
panther cub license/food	$900.00

EDUCATION	
magic lessons	$500.00
Champagne room playdates	$1,200.00
private laser tag tutor	$ 0.00
	(but have to buy cigarettes and nudie mags for tutor upon request)

CHILD CARE	
salary for full-time smokin' hot nanny	$3,000.00
meals for full-time smokin' hot nanny	$400.00
cost of acquiring/preventing green card for full-time smokin' hot nanny	$10,000.00
	(campaign donations)
legal fees for fighting outlandish harassment charges levied by full-time smokin' hot nanny	$65,625.00
hush money for full-time smokin' hot nanny when legal defense fails	$5,000.00
TOTAL MONTHLY BABY EXPENSES	**$107,000.73**

SELECTING A MATE

ne way or the other you're going to need a member of the opposite gender in order to produce a child. While most conception comes through banging, or "coitus," oftentimes the person you most want to coitus is not an ideal mate. This is due to three primary factors:

1. **GENETICS**

   Your child will receive 50% of his DNA from you and 50% from your partner. That means that no matter how totally awesome you are, the best you can possibly hope for is a half-awesome kid if you hump a total dud. That's why even Kevin Federline's kids are a mess.

2. **COMPATABILITY**

   Legally or otherwise you will be linked with your partner for the entirety of your child's life. This can lead to serious trouble if he speaks a different language, espouses antiquated values, lacks a high school education, or—if he happens to be from Kansas—all of the above.

3. **HOTNESS**

   As discussed in *The Bro Code* and other literary works of significance, hot people tend to be crazier, meaner, and dumber than the average person. Ironically, the very same qualities that make them so attractive are precisely what make them poor parents. Except for big boobs. That's a win-win for everyone.

As you go about deciding whether to have a kid, make sure you factor in *who* you're going to have a kid with. Whether you're out on the prowl or currently in a relationship, you might want to carry around this handy list and make sure any potential partners check all the boxes before you check *their* box (what up?!).

PARENTING PARTNER CHECKLIST

You want to have sex with him/her. ☐

And would even if you were sober. ☐

And even after he/she packs on 20–30 pounds. ☐

He/She seems rich. ☐

He/She is taller than five foot four (nobody likes a short person). ☐

He/She has not mentioned the Resurrection in the last fifteen seconds. ☐

He/She looks like he/she could produce a professional sports star, tech entrepreneur, or tristate lottery winner. ☐

You still want to bang him/her. ☐

He/She seems like someone who's more interested in changing diapers than you are. ☐

He/She is not a member of your family or does not look enough like you that he/she might conceivably be revealed later as your long-lost cousin. ☐

He/She is not currently wearing any NASCAR memorabilia. ☐

His/Her full name does *not* sound like that of a serial killer. ☐

THE SCIENCE

Unfortunately there is no strong scientific consensus on where babies come from. The latest theory posits that babies emerge from a vagina and not in fact from a handkerchief delivered by a stork, but nobody has yet been able to prove it. We simply lack the technological ability at this time to shrink ourselves down to a size where we can fully explore the intricacies of the female reproductive system.*

Because human reproduction exists largely as a frontier science, we must rely on complicated, hypothetical models. Since the scientific jargon can get confusing and boring, I've boiled the most popular theory down to an easy-to-understand format.

---

* Preliminary efforts are under way, however. If you'd like to learn more, I urge you to watch the excellent documentary *Innerspace*, starring Dennis Quaid, Martin Short, and a human-faced Meg Ryan.

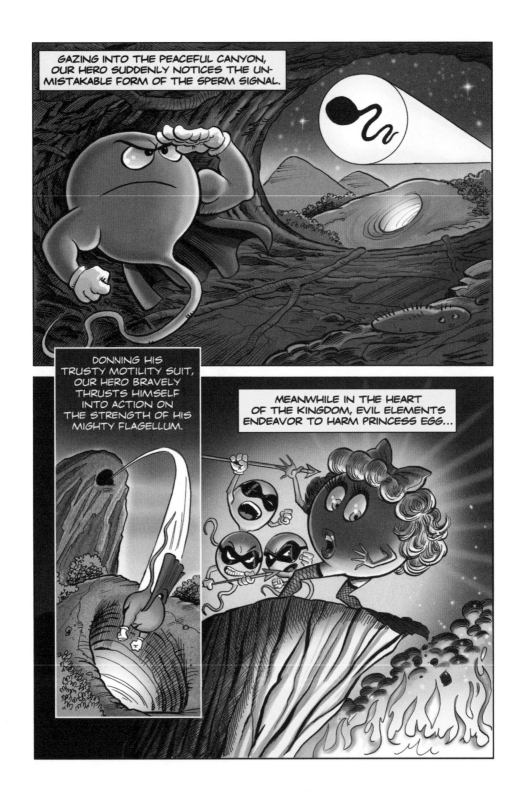

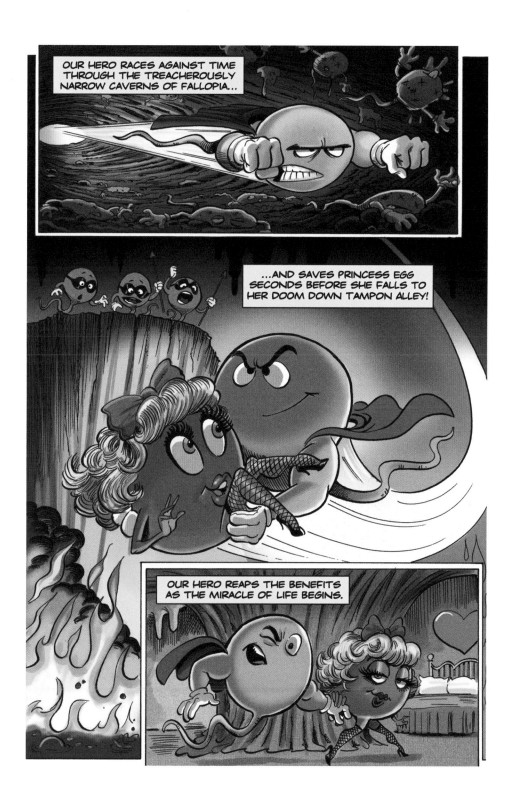

TIMING

According to science a baby is born roughly thirty-eight weeks after conception. (And I do mean "roughly.") That means you actually have some semblance of control over when your child is born. As such, you'll need to act responsibly and practice safe sex if you want to ensure your due date doesn't coincide with an important and immovable conflict like your annual Vegas trip with the guys.

The best family planning begins with forward thinking. With that in mind you'll want to avoid banging in late March, since nobody wants to waste their valuable Christmas vacation in a hospital dropping off tacky flowers and pretending your newborn *doesn't* look like a shrunken Don Rickles.

You'll also want to do everything humanly possible to avoid a due date smack-dab in the middle of the NFL season. The last thing you want is your kid to do an Internet search and discover that on the sacred, magical day of her birth you took the time to go online and mock your fantasy opponent for starting Adrian Peterson despite the season-ending ACL injury he sustained the previous week . . . I mean seriously, all it takes is five minutes of online research before the games start, Ted.

To help plan your birth around an acceptable due date, here are a few key "don't" dates.

CONCEPTION CALENDAR

DON'T DO IT DATE	DUE DATE	DILEMMA
January 31	Halloween	Confusing actual nurse for chick in slutty nurse costume could be embarrassing/actionable.
fourth Thursday of February	Thanksgiving	If you have to scoop anything out from between trussed-up legs on this day it better be stuffing.
March 21	Adult Video News Awards	Newborn child easily upstaged by other naked humans.
April 1	New Year's	Good luck getting a cab to the hospital.
first week in May	Super Bowl	If your team is playing, you will *never* forgive your child, win or lose.
May 24	Oscars	Hard to comment on red carpet fashion disasters when you're wearing hospital booties, your husband's "car washing" shirt, and a hairstyle held in place by amniotic fluid.
June 15–July 1	March Madness	Come on, Bro.
June 17	St. Paddy's Day	The only bodily fluids you should be cleaning up on this sacred day are your own.
July 3	*Game of Thrones* season premiere	You could watch it later, but then you'll have nothing to talk about at work.
October 4	Fourth of July	You're really going to blow the long weekend on this?

The
Giving
it
up
Tree

by

Barney
StinsonStein

GETTING LUCKY . . . ER

For whatever reason, getting knocked up isn't a sure thing even if your partner is. There's no guarantee you'll get pregnant despite perfect timing, sperm that could blast through granite, and eggs so fertile they'd make a fundamentalist Mormon woman blush were she allowed to do so without permission.

The irony is that this very uncertainty used to be your best friend. How many times have you gotten down on your hands and knees and thanked the heavens they didn't punish you for getting down on your hands and knees? Of course now that you're actually trying to get pregnant and not preparing to flee the country at the first hint of a late period, it suddenly seems like the hardest thing in the world . . . well, second hardest (Hello!).

The important thing is not to panic—just because you're not pregnant after hours or even days of banging doesn't mean you have an abandoned drive-in theater of a uterus or your sperm is the Olympic equivalent of Eric Moussambani—the swimmer from Equatorial Guinea who I believe is still trying to finish the 100m freestyle at the 2000 Sydney games. As frustrating as it might seem at times, all you can do is keep plugging away at plugging away.

As the months go on, it may start to feel like sex is a job and you'll be tempted to give up or move to the Netherlands where you can at least make an honest living at it. If it is getting stale, try spicing things up by using my sexual role-playing generator—the only role-playing generator currently certified for use by the strict Thai Adult Film Society.

SEXUAL ROLE-PLAYING GENERATOR

Roll the die for each category, assemble your props and costumes, and let your imaginations run wild. As an example, if a lucky girl and I were to roll a 4, 2, 1, 6, 3, 4, we would simply procure a boomerang and a skateboard, dress up as a firefighter and a sumo wrestler, and have the "birds and bees" talk while seductively working in the phrase, "Yep. You've got termites." Note: For best results try capturing the evening on video.

PROP 1	PROP 2	COSTUME 1	COSTUME 2	SCENARIO	SEXY LINE
plunger	medicine ball	firefighter	samurai warrior	Census taker approaches shut-in	"Bottle or tap?"
pogo stick	skateboard	19th-century deep-sea diver	competitive cyclist	Employee requests a raise	"If you think it's so cool, then you can smoke the whole pack."
pool skimmer	Confederate musket	fighter pilot	Philly phanatic	"Birds and bees" discussion	"Any idea how fast you were driving?"
boomerang	stuffed grizzly bear	Santa Claus	robot	Drive-thru window transaction	"Yep. You've got termites."
Ping-Pong paddle	2-tray tackle box	pirate	Girl scout	News anchor banters with field reporter	"Crust on or crust off?"
life preserver	bassoon	rodeo clown	sumo wrestler	Neighbors dispute property line	"He got a two-strike hanger and deposited it in the leftfield bleachers."

TELLING POP

Finding out you're pregnant is the most exciting discovery you will ever make, next to stumbling upon one of those conjoined peanut M&M's or learning that your cable package includes the Romanian Spice Channel. No matter how you slice it, that little "positive" sign means your life is about to change in significant ways, beginning with a welcome break from having to mount that bloated mess of flesh you call a husband.

You'll be tempted to immediately tweet the news to everyone—your parents, your friends, that girl from the neighboring cubicle who's been following your journey with the creepy zealotry only an acne-ridden cat breeder can know—but prudence dictates you should wait. Plus, it's time to tell the father-to-be, and like so many urine-soaked sticks before him, you'll need to handle it delicately.

It's best to tell the father in person since reading a text that says, "I'm preggers!" may knock him right off his motorcycle. You'll want to pick a time when he's not relatively preoccupied. For example, if one of his teams is in the playoffs, you should wait until after they win. If they lose, it's best to wait until after he's done smashing the end table to pieces with an ax.

Fellas, do your best to remain calm and collected when you hear the news. Women are very sensitive to body language and you don't want to make her nervous by immediately going pale and projectile-vomiting all over yourself.

To make sure you're expressing a supportive attitude no matter what you're feeling inside, simply follow my Emotional Translator.

EMOTIONAL TRANSLATOR

WHAT YOU WANT TO SAY	WHAT YOU SHOULD SAY
"Hmm, I guess someone's not buying himself a new ski boat after all."	"Great! That's great news! Just . . . great."
"Remember Erica? The ex-girlfriend who was decidedly more liberal in the bedroom? How come *she* never got pregnant? Huh?!"	"I can't believe it! That's amazing! We should celebrate! Got any ideas?"
"Unsubscribe."	"Awesome!"
"I suppose now she'll want to use the spare room as a nursery and not as a repository for the rare Star Wars memorabilia I've only been collecting *my entire life*!"	"That's wonderful, honey! Gee, are we gonna have enough room? Maybe we should think about getting a bigger place . . ."
"$*@&!!!!!!!!!!!!!!!!!!!!!"	"Wow! Can you give me a minute to go outside and process this life-altering moment? If you don't mind, I'm gonna take this end table and ax out with me."

HOW DO YOU KNOW IF YOU'RE PREGNANT?

Simple. You get fat, girl! Just kidding, though you're definitely going to pork out at some point. The good news is that our ability to determine pregnancy has been steadily improving since the Neolithic Age, when you wouldn't find out until a screaming baby dropped out and ruined an otherwise perfectly pleasant gathering session with the gals. While surprise births still happen today in isolated pockets of the world where they find those geniuses who appear on *I Didn't Know I Was Pregnant*, reliable pregnancy tests have been around for thousands of years.

In ancient Egypt women would urinate into a container filled with barley seeds and wheat grains. If they sprouted, she was pregnant. If not, at least they had a pretty hoppy keg of beer to enjoy after a long day of pyramid building. Fortunately, because of significant advances in modern technology, there are far more accurate devices for women to pee on.

Today's pregnancy tests range from home-based kits to a rosette inhibition assay—a clinical exam that tests for "early pregnancy factor" or EPF.* The good news is that the significantly more affordable home-based kits are approximately 75% accurate, or when used by people who understand that only the woman is supposed to pee on it, 96%.

---

* EPF is not to be confused with EMF, the early nineties pop band that brought us the smash hit "Unbelievable," which when played is, ironically, one of the most effective forms of birth control.

UNEXPECTED PREGNANCIES

I'd like to take a moment to discuss a touchy subject: unexpected pregnancies. They can happen to anyone, not just characters in a daytime television show or the Bible. They can even happen to dudes, as we learned eighteen years ago when Emma Thompson knocked up Arnold Schwarzenegger. True story.

Unfortunately it doesn't take much for a "happy accident" to quickly destroy an otherwise healthy relationship. All it takes is one offhanded suggestion that she's been boning that orange guy Eric from the gym and suddenly it's World War III.

To help avoid this ugly scenario, I'd like to address men and women separately with the hope that you'll be able to calmly work through this and emerge a stronger, healthier couple and maybe, just maybe, a family.

FOR HER

It's time to sit down and review your ethical beliefs, your financial situation, and overall emotional health. Are you ready to be a responsible, loving parent? Is this the man you want to father your child? Have you gotten everything you need out of this Eric?

If you're certain you're ready then you'll need to carefully broach the subject with the father. It's best to begin with a reaffirmation of your feelings for him and then patiently explain the situation. Let him process the information, and do your best not to quickly judge any involuntary facial or bodily reactions he might have. Tell him you understand that he'll need some time to decide whether a child is something he's really ready for and agree to revisit the topic when he's thought it through.

FOR HIM

Immediately deny that it's yours. She'll need a paternity test and you'll be long gone before that ever happens or at the very least well situated for a guest spot on Maury Povich's show.

COMPLICATIONS

f you're still not pregnant after months or even years of trying, you might be encountering a setback more serious than any amount of emotional fatigue, sexual malaise, or scrotal chafing . . . I'm talking, of course, about infertility. If you're facing infertility, there are a number of possible solutions:

1. SURROGATE

    Some women will essentially rent you their uterus. Be sure to pick a woman who is healthy, emotionally stable, and not quite hot enough that Daddy will be tempted to take her vagina out for a little test drive.

2. ADOPTION

    Many mothers realize after giving birth that they simply don't have the resources to take care of a child and will offer him up for adoption. While interviewing with an adoption agency can be a lengthy and expensive process here in the United States, there are deals to be had if you're okay bagging a kid from a developing nation. You'll probably have to go there to get him though, because many of those countries have unreliable postal services.

4. SPERM BRONOR

    If it's a male issue, you can acquire another dude's baby gravy by finding a sperm donor, or "sperm bronor." Since you're essentially looking for a guy to genetically bang your wife, it makes sense to screen for things like disease, personality, and overall awesomeness. If one of your buddies fits the bill, you can either pursue the expensive medical process of collection and implantation or, if you're feeling generous, slap a blindfold on your wife, and tag in your Bro during date night. The choice is yours.

If you're looking for the ultimate sperm bronor, I can deliver my own genetically superior gametes right to your womb-step. Please have the prospective mother fill out and submit the following questionnaire for consideration.

APPLICATION FOR
BARNEY STINSON'S SUPER SPERM

1. With 1 being "petrified log" and 10 being "human slinky," how flexible are you?

   1   2   3   4   5   6   7   8   9   1 0

2. Have you previously been described as a "screamer"?   ❏ Yes   ❏ No

3. Would your husband/boyfriend be willing to operate a video camera during
   the implantation procedure?   ❏ Yes   ❏ No

4. If logistic purposes make it more expedient, would you mind going back-to-back
   with another applicant?   ❏ Yes   ❏ No

5. How about front-to-front?   ❏ Yes   ❏ No

6. Are you able to pay the $5,000 fee in cash?   ❏ Yes   ❏ No

7. Wait, you don't expect me to be involved in the child's life, do you?   ❏ No

8. If I were on a wild animal safari, what animal would you be and what would you do to me?

   _____

9. How likely will you be to sign the following affidavit: "Barney Stinson is the biggest and most
   satisfying lover I've ever been with. You should totally bang him."

   ❏ Somewhat Likely   ❏ Likely   ❏ Very Likely   ❏ Like Totally Likely

10. In the space provided, please attach a recent, full-body picture of yourself washing a hot rod.

PART II

YOU'RE PREGNANT . . .
NOW WHAT?

Congratulations! You now have a human being growing inside you. During the next nine months this creature will siphon your precious bodily nutrients, expand your stomach to the size of a diving bell, and pack on seven or more pounds before finally blasting through your uterine wall and into the world.

The good news is that there are actually plenty of things to look forward to during this special period of your life:

- **NAMING**
  Many people don't realize it, but you, and not the hospital, get to choose a name for your child. I hear "Barney" is a popular option for both boys and girls.

- **PIGGING OUT**
  Now that you're eating for two, you can stuff almost anything down your gullet and nobody will blink an eye. This will be the only time

in your life you will be allowed and encouraged to consume a bacon, cheese, and Oreo milkshake through a corn dog straw.

■ BOOB GROWTH

Something both you and the father will enjoy together is the natural swelling of your gazongas, which can increase in cup size by as many as two to three letters. Best of all? Your new and improved squeeze bags won't cost you a dime! Downside? Once the kid's out, those knockers fall to the ground faster than a poorly constructed paper airplane.

Unfortunately not all the changes will be positive. During your pregnancy you will gain substantial weight, your feet will flatten into the shape and density of a cast-iron skillet, and the skin on your face will take on the glossy sheen of a hardboiled egg . . . Basically, you'll be lucky to come out of this thing looking like the Stay Puft Marshmallow Man.

Congratulations!

TIMELINE

Much like a hockey game, your pregnancy is divided into three periods that, also like a hockey game, last about three months each. These "trimesters" serve as useful landmarks that are roughly characterized as follows:

First trimester = "cranky"
Second trimester = "glowing"
Third trimester = "crap-your-maternity-pants"

On the following page is a timeline that charts the changes your body will go through as your baby grows during the pregnancy.

4 WEEKS

The heart and spinal column have begun to form and your child is approximately ¹⁄₂₅ of an inch tall. To put that in perspective, it would take over one hundred of your children standing on each other's unformed shoulders to equal the height of Tom Cruise.

8 WEEKS

Your child's heart has begun to beat at a regular rhythm and his sexual organs have started to develop . . . though it will be twelve years before he starts beating *them* at a regular rhythm.

12–20 WEEKS

Your baby grows to 5 inches in length and closes its eyelids . . . presumably to shield itself from the sight of your grotesquely expanding stomach.

20–32 WEEKS

The baby tests its newly formed fingers and toenails with powerful jabs and kicks to your sensitive internal organs. Not really a Bro move, fetus!

32–40 WEEKS

With her lungs fully formed, the baby focuses on packing on the pounds and rotating her stubble-coated, arrow-shaped head downward in preparation for cannonballing out of your vagina.

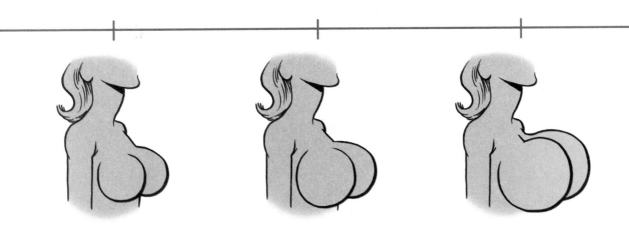

29

BABYMOON

Now that you're pregnant, you might want to plan a trip so the two of you can enjoy some time together before the baby arrives. Traveling with diapers, food, toys, and breast pumps is almost impossible . . . now imagine doing it with a baby and all of *her* crap!

Since your ability to relax and unwind will vanish the second your baby is born, I recommend taking the most irresponsible trip you can afford. For more information on where to go and how best to spend your time, stay tuned for my forthcoming travel guide series.

Lets Bro
Europe
by Barney Stinson

MORNING SICKNESS

During your first trimester it's not uncommon to experience "morning sickness"—mild to violent nausea brought about by changes to your bio-chemistry. In many ways morning sickness is just like a hangover, from the intermittent waves of queasiness, to the ceaseless vomiting, to the overall regret of what you did to feel this way.

Because of these similarities you can help combat morning sickness with some simple hangover remedies:

- Keep a water bottle or sports drink by the bed to prevent dehydration. (You should be in the habit of doing this anyway if you have even half a clue of what you're doing in the sack.)
- Pig out with a bunch of greasy food. If a restaurant offers chili, be sure to slather it over everything, including another bowl of chili.
- Wear sunglasses everywhere you go to limit glare and generally look awesome.
- Employ the "hair of the dog" strategy by getting pregnant again.
- A few hits from the bong probably aren't going to hurt anyone.
- Conceal a plastic bag in your purse so you can barf in public while "searching for your keys."
- Park yourself in a sauna or hot tub for a few hours.
- Four words: *Law & Order* marathon.
- Fill a Ziploc bag with coconut water, attach a straw to it, then jam the straw into the largest vein you can find to create your own IV drip.
- Sweat it out with three to four hundred crunches.*†

* Editor's note: I'm pretty sure advice like this is the worst thing possible for a pregnant woman.
† Author's note: I'm pretty sure comments like this are why you'll never be a pregnant woman. Oh no he didn't!!!! Sorry, that was uncalled for. You're doing a great job, Editor. Really.

ANNOUNCING THE NEWS

As tempting as it might be to tell everyone that you're pregnant, it's important to be discreet when disseminating the information. Just like when you bang the hot flight attendant on your flight from Miami to New York there's a right time, place, and way to share the news . . . For me it was individually as my fellow passengers exited the plane so I could actually point her out.

Here's a flowchart that will help you figure out who to tell and when.

IMMEDIATELY . . .

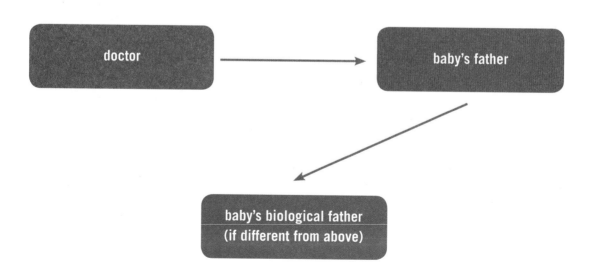

THREE MONTHS LATER . . .

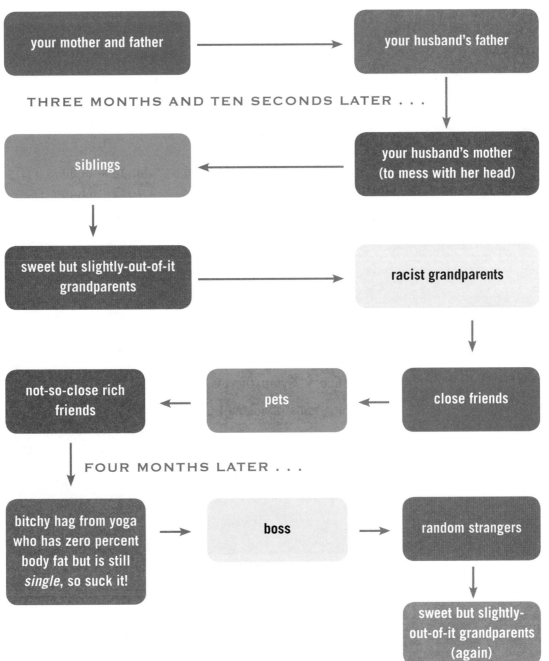

| your mother and father | → | your husband's father |

THREE MONTHS AND TEN SECONDS LATER . . .

siblings ← your husband's mother (to mess with her head)

sweet but slightly-out-of-it grandparents → racist grandparents

not-so-close rich friends ← pets ← close friends

FOUR MONTHS LATER . . .

bitchy hag from yoga who has zero percent body fat but is still *single*, so suck it! → boss → random strangers → sweet but slightly-out-of-it grandparents (again)

THE SWEET SPOT

One of the few joys of pregnancy is the free boob job. In preparation for breastfeeding, your cans will immediately start growing. Some have been known to swell by as much as four or five handfuls each. Unfortunately you won't get to enjoy your new rack for very long because within a few weeks your tummy will soon catch up and ultimately leave you bloated like a Thanksgiving Day parade balloon. So now's the time to try on that coconut bra or model at a gun show or bang your ta-tas like a couple of congas while listening to the start of the Rolling Stones' "Sympathy for the Devil." You should also take as many photographs of yourself as possible because you will never be this hot again. Ever. In fact, many experts recommend staging and shooting your family photo now since you can always Photoshop the kid in later.

DIET

By now you've probably heard a lot of outrageous claims about food, like you can't eat fish when you're pregnant because of dangerously high mercury levels. That's just a lot of tin-foil-hat hooey, like when someone says if you cross your eyes, they'll freeze like that or that masturbation causes blindness or when a "doctor" points to numbers on your "liver panel" and says unless you stop drinking three cases of energy drink a day, it's only a matter of time until you experience "systemic renal failure."

Basically you should feel free to ingest anything you want. The only things to avoid are alcohol, drugs, and roller coasters . . . In short, if it sounds like fun, avoid it.

EDITOR'S NOTE: This is a good place to remind readers about the legal disclaimer in the front of this book, which clearly and openly states that any "advice" dispensed within these pages is devoid of scientific evidence, medical substance, and in this case, common sense.

AUTHOR'S NOTE: It seems like we have a sexy, Sam-and-Diane kind of thing going on here, Editor. You know, where we disagree on everything because deep down, we really dig each other. We should bang. Thoughts?

EDITOR'S NOTE: No.

TIME CAPSULE

As you prepare your home for the baby by ruthlessly tossing away anything that could be deemed "unsafe" by a county or state official, you might wish to set aside any items you won't be able to use when the baby arrives and lock them away in a time capsule. Years later, when you've finally shipped the bastard off to college or war, you can crack open the capsule and rediscover your awesome pre-baby existence. Some sentimental items to consider:

- sex toys
- weaponry
- sporting goods
- weekends
- musical instruments
- motorcycle/convertible/boat
- bong
- inflatable pornography
- cash
- any pants that aren't sweatpants

THE BOOBS ON THE BUS

The boobs on the bus go up and down. Up and down. Up and down. The boobs on the bus go up and down, All through the town!

The people on the bus go, "What's that smell?"
"What's that smell?"
"What's that smell?"
The people on the bus go, "What's that smell?"
All through the town!

The cell phones on the bus go beep beep beep.
Beep beep beep.
Beep beep beep.
The cell phones on the bus go beep beep beep,
If they get a signal!

The driver on the bus mutters, "Kill me now."
"Kill me now."
"Kill me now."
The driver on the bus mutters, "Kill me now,"
All through the town!

The nut-job on the bus goes, "Ha ha ha!"
"Ha ha ha!"
"Ha ha ha!"
The nut-job on the bus goes, "Ha ha ha!"
All through the town!

The hipsters on the bus go pfft pfft pfft.
Pfft pfft pfft.
Pfft pfft pfft.
The hipsters on the bus go pfft pfft pfft,
All the way to a crappy gallery!

The junkie on the bus goes shoot shoot shoot.
Shoot shoot shoot.
Shoot shoot shoot.
The junkie on the bus goes shoot shoot shoot,
All through the town.

The hemophiliac on the bus goes squirt squirt squirt.
Squirt squirt squirt.
Squirt squirt squirt.
The hemophiliac on the bus goes squirt squirt squirt,
All through the town.

The mugger on the bus goes, "Keep quiet and you'll live."
"Keep quiet and you'll live."
"Keep quiet and you'll live."
The mugger on the bus goes, "Keep quiet and you'll live,"
All through the town!

FEATHERING YOUR NEST
OF AWESOMENESS

ne of the more fun endeavors you will undertake is preparing the nursery. You'll want to take great care, as this will be your child's first bachelor's pad or chick's coop © (copyright pending, Barney Stinson, 2012).

The first thing you'll need to do is "baby-proof" your entire home, which simply means clearing out the hundreds of pairs of shoes you're never going to wear (ladies) and the hundreds of pounds of porn you've cleverly "hidden" over the years (fellas . . . and ladies too, I assume). Next you'll need to purchase lots and lots of crap.

As you can see, baby prep starts to get expensive. The good news is you can save money by creatively repurposing items from your single life.

- That giant box of condoms you eagerly purchased for your trip to Hedonism can finally be put to use as 144 latex footies.
- The R2-D2 cooler you stole from the 7-Eleven makes a handy diaper disposal unit. ("R2-D-Poo"? Umm . . . Billion Dollar Idea Alert! Are you listening, Mr. Lucas???)
- Unused diaphragm? Take a magic marker to it and slap it on your child's noggin as a festive beanie.

CRAP YOU HAVE TO BUY

CRAP	ESTIMATED COST
playpen	$200.00
crib	$500.00
baby's first tanning bed	$4,700.00
coroner-level stainless steel changing table	$850.00
bottles	$60.00
nipples (heh)	$30.00
"baby monitors" (PRC-3088 military-band tactical transceivers you can use later during laser tag)	$ 1,375.00
leather massage glider	$ 4,350.00
cute stuffed animal	FREE Steal from friend (Ted)
fiber-optic camera to go in stuffed animal's eye—for breastfeeding/nanny-peeping	$ 349.99
Total	$ 12,414.99

Lastly, you can save a lot of dough by making your own decorations. As my first gift to you (other than the wealth of knowledge presented in these pages), I'd like to give your child an awesome-themed mobile. Simply cut out the images below and hang them from the ceiling above your little loved one's head.

DOCTOR

One of the first things you need to do after getting knocked up is to choose an ob-gyn, or "lady doctor." You need to find someone that both you and the father are comfortable with. Why? Because for the next nine months this stranger's going to be poking all around your mess.

As you interview doctors, an important consideration is how quickly she can get you through labor. A long birth means missing sporting events, losing some of your precious nap time, and coughing up a lot of dough, since hospitals, like fine hotels, charge by the hour.

To help you pick an ob-gyn who fits your needs, feel free to use the attached questionnaire.

OB-GYN INTERROGATION

1. Your diploma says you attended _____ University. Impressive! So, since you really did attend _____ University, you shouldn't have any trouble recalling what their mascot is, right? And how exactly does the fight song go again?

2. Do you have any reservations about prescribing or administering pain relief medication to me?

3. Do you have any reservations about prescribing or administering pain relief medication to my husband/boyfriend?

4. What percentage of your births require a cesarean section?

5. And what exactly is a cesarean section?

6. Really? Good Lord! Well, if you determine that birth conditions require you to perform a cesarean, are you willing to yank out some fat while you're in there?

7. On television you always see babies being born in stuck elevators. Does that really ever happen?

8. Can you assure my husband/boyfriend that this birth will not leave me with a "billowy tent flap" down there?

9. My husband/boyfriend would like to know if he can cut the umbilical cord with a giant pair of novelty scissors like the mayor uses during a ribbon cutting ceremony.

10. Is it okay to film it? We'd love to share the joyous moment of our child's birth with our treasured friends and family . . . especially since we already shared with them the video of our child's conception. We can forward you the link, it's pretty hot.

SEX

ewly pregnant couples have a lot of questions about sex. Let's see what Dr. Barney has to say . . .

Q: *Is it really safe for us to have sex?*

A: Studies have shown it's A-OK to get it on with your partner. What studies haven't shown is whether it's okay to have sex with other people. That said, it's best to err on the side of caution and get it in now wherever you can.

Q: *This may sound silly, but my penis won't hurt the baby, will it?*

A: *Yours* won't . . .

Q: *I suddenly feel less attracted to my partner. Is that normal?*

A: Yes. It's perfectly normal to lose your passion for a person who, despite bigger breasts, has become increasingly irritable, falls asleep at random moments, and has ballooned to the size and shape of a coastal marine mammal. To be fair, *he* may not find you so attractive right now either.

Q: *Is it safe for me to orgasm?*

A: Studies have shown that it's not only safe for the male to reach orgasm but healthy for the baby if he does so multiple times, preferably without much effort on his part and while watching TV. As far as the pregnant female goes, it's unfortunately very unsafe for her to orgasm. (You owe me, Bro.)

Q: *I'm a little embarrassed asking this, but is it safe for my husband to perform oral sex on me?*

A: Ooooh, I'm afraid not. An air bubble could block a blood vessel and create an embolism and thereby endanger the child. In fact, even after you give birth, you should probably just avoid cunnilingus altogether, you know, to play it safe. (Seriously. I'm hitting nothing but solid line drives for you, buddy.)

EDUCATION

If, for some reason, you think you need more help than what's provided in this informative text, there are other, significantly less awesome, educational options.

CHILDBIRTH CLASSES

These classes primarily teach you how to handle the ungodly amounts of pain you will face during labor. They're traditionally held in a group setting with other doomed couples and provide both important facts about childbirth as well as useless garbage about relationships, mental health, and other borderline witchcraft.

MIDWIFE

If you'd rather have your own, personal coach guide you through the process, you can consider hiring something called a midwife. As best I can tell, when scary situations arise like the baby stops kicking or you run out of fudge ripple, the midwife is there to help.

MOVIES

If you are more of a visual learner, there are many instructional films that can help you prepare for the realities of pregnancy and life with a newborn.

Three Men and a Baby   *Look Who's Talking*
Look Who's Talking Too   *Apocalypse Now*
Insomnia   *Die Hard* (not really, but should be on every movie list)
Honey, I Shrunk the Kids   *Alien*
Twins   *Titanic* (The boat is a metaphor for your body.)

GOING FURTHER:
WHAT IS A MIDWIFE?

To be honest, I'm not really sure what a midwife is. When I first heard someone mention "the midwife," I thought maybe it was a crappy cable drama starring a former A-list actress on the wrong side of forty like Julia Roberts or Lindsay Lohan. But the more I think about it, *The Midwife* sounds like it could be a gritty suspense film in which a crazed and scantily clad Angelina Jolie lustily tracks down and kills her ex-husband's first and third wives . . . You know, it's set in a small Southern town and at first everyone suspects the husband (let's say Ryan Gosling for the ladies). With Gosling in jail, we introduce an "evil stepmother" dynamic when Angelina takes custody of his daughter after the death of the third wife (Anne Hathaway . . . we know she's great in death scenes after seeing her host the Oscars). Just when it seems the case is closed, the detective with the drinking problem or stutter (Philip Seymour Hoffman?) starts to wonder if Angelina is involved. When he goes to question her, she seduces him, stabs him in the eye with a rusty boat cleat, and stuffs him in a fish locker (let's make it a sleepy New England village, but have the director—Francis Ford Coppola—tell everyone to take it easy on the accents). Meanwhile, Ryan Gosling finds a confidante in the quirky yet principled sheriff's deputy, Sandra Bullock. (If we get the note "too many brunettes," we can always young up the role with Emma Stone or bust the budget with Charlize Theron . . . though maybe it's just me, but it always takes me out of it when she plays a public servant.) They bond over the necklace Gosling's daughter made for him and eventually Bullock/Stone/Theron overcomes her restrictive righteousness and lets him out of jail even though it could come at the expense of her badge, which is a big deal to her because she promised her dead father (Albert Finney or Denzel Washington) she'd be sheriff one day. When they show up to rescue the stepdaughter, Angelina tries to escape by walking out on a treacherous sea cliff. Gosling goes after her but she falls into the frigid and unforgiving Atlantic. We pan up from the waves to see the sun rising three years later on Bullock/Stone/Theron and Gosling walking on the beach as a married couple. As Gosling runs off to take the stepdaughter to hockey practice, Bullock/Stone/Theron notices something shiny wash up on the sand—Gosling's necklace! Did he push Angelina off that cliff three years ago? Did he kill all his wives? Is Bullock/Stone/Theron next?

Anyway, that's a midwife.

BABY SHOWER

At a certain point one of your friends will become obsessed with planning your baby shower. Sadly it won't be your closest friend, it'll be your raspy-throated, "big-boned" friend who's constantly on the verge of breaking down in tears or getting up on her reinforced soapbox to complain about how there are no good guys out there.

She will either plan a coed shower—where a bunch of guys who don't want to be there on a Saturday afternoon try desperately to get drunk on mimosas—or a more traditional "female-only" shower—where a bunch of chicks in thousand-dollar outfits pretend they don't hate each other, eat chocolate bars out of diapers, and try desperately to get drunk on mimosas.

BABY SHOWER FAQS

What should Daddy do during the baby shower if it's not coed?
Bachelor Party Part Deux. Since you don't have to be there, you and your Bros should take the time to gamble, blow crap up, or indulge in any other culturally enriching activity. Note: If you have any single Bros, have them "accidentally" show up at the baby shower. A baby shower is basically the adult equivalent of a sorority pillow fight and an excellent place to pick off chicks made horny by the inescapable cocktail of jealousy, desperation, chocolate . . . and actual cocktails.

How many gifts should I register for?

As many as you possibly can. This is also a golden opportunity to sneak in some higher-priced items that have nothing to do with the baby. For example, you can easily slip in a new flat-screen TV between a turtle-shaped baby bouncer and a diaper bag covered in blushing endangered animals.

Should I open the gifts in front of everyone?

No! Avoid this at all costs. Studies have shown that opening gifts at a baby shower takes more time than it took for the Himalayas to form. That's why the Wise Men came late and only brought three unwrapped items. If a zealous guest insists that you open the ironic mustache pacifiers he brought, do so privately, preferably near a trash can. If others approach with gifts outstretched like a herd of acknowledgment-thirsty zombies, you can always feign illness, pull the fire alarm, or pretend you're going into labor.

Do I have to invite my "handsy" boss?

Yup.

LIFE INSURANCE/ GUARDIANSHIP

Now that you have a child, it's a good idea to purchase life insurance. As responsible parents you need to plan ahead so that your child will have the resources to lead the awesome life you wanted to give her, even if you both go down trying out your homemade flying squirrel suits, taking a run at the couple's breath-holding world record, or in a hail of gunfire while attempting a sweet-ass bank robbery like the one at the end of *Heat*.

Now is also a good time to discuss guardianship. Sadly, I'm kinda busy right now, so you'll have to choose someone you know personally. Given that most people you know personally are either your family or your friends, it's likely to be a lose-lose type of choice.

The best way to choose someone is through the process of elimination. Simply follow the flowchart below to determine your child's legal guardian.

HOW TO PICK A GUARDIAN

ELIMINATE	REASON
everyone who makes less than $250,000 a year	You want someone with enough financial liquidity to afford a top-notch education, an emergency medical procedure, or—heaven forbid—an afternoon at Disney World.
both sets of parents	Remember how much they sucked as parents?
any friends who already have five or more kids of their own	Your kid is likely to get ignored or, worse, roped into some sort of weird, incestuous family band where she'll be forced to play the tambourine and wear costumes made out of drapery.
your hot friends	As Confucius says, "The road to mental instability begins with masturbating to your legal guardian."
Ted	I'm taller and way better-looking than him.

COMMUNICATION

Many so-called experts believe you can communicate with your child even though she's crammed deep inside your stomach. I suppose it's possible, given the number of heated disagreements I've had with Thai food.

The truth is you can start talking to your child right from the get-go. Obviously you should take great care in what you say. For example, I don't recommend regaling your fetus with ribald tales of your greatest bangs . . . That's better served ex utero when your child can actually see you act out the various positions and facial expressions.

Studies have shown that, in addition to speaking to your child, exposing your child to music at an early age may increase her intelligence. Since you want to give your child the biggest advantage possible, I recommend jamming a speaker against your stomach and cranking up Van Halen's *1984*.

Experts also believe that reading aloud to your unborn child encourages bonding by introducing him to the sound of your voice. It's also an excellent way to kick-start your child's education. Take turns with your partner reading from some of the following fundamental works, available wherever awesome books are sold:

Everyone you know will want to feel the baby move around, but let's face it: it's a little creepy to have relative strangers grope you free of charge. Instead, encourage them to offer your child a light fist bump.

MILKING YOUR PREGNANCY

Most people mistakenly believe that you can't nurse until after you give birth, but did you know you can actually start milking right now? People will move mountains for a pregnant chick and now's your chance to take advantage of their, frankly, sexist hospitality.

AT WORK

Covet a colleague's parking space or office? Well, guess what? Now that you're pregnant, you need to park closer to the building and require easy access to the kitchen or the bathroom or the precious, life-sustaining vitamin D that only the sunlight in that bitch Debra's corner office can supply.

AT THE GROCERY STORE

You should be able to cajole a legion of pimply-faced adolescents to follow you in a grocery cart convoy as you pillage the store's candy and chip aisle. This is also an excellent opportunity to stuff your shirt with pricey sirloin like they used to do on *Supermarket Sweep*, because really, what grocery store manager has the balls to question your oddly angular pregnant stomach?

OUT TO EAT

Tired of waiting for your meal to arrive at a restaurant? Simply survey the room for a tasty-looking dish and point to it while rubbing your stomach. By law you are entitled to that food since you're eating for two now. Remember, if you don't like it, you can always exchange it for someone else's meal at no charge.

IN TRAFFIC

You know when you play Grand Theft Auto for twenty-nine hours straight and then get in your car and have a hard time *not* driving on the sidewalk? Well now's your chance to finally do it! Just roll down the window and intermittently shout out "I'm in labor!" as you plow through parks and careen through poorly positioned fruit stands.

AT THE AIRPORT

I'm no TSA official, but it certainly sounds unhealthy for a pregnant woman to walk through an X-ray machine. This is your once-in-a-lifetime opportunity to smuggle in as many water bottles, aerosol deodorant cans, and class C fireworks as you can cram in your maternity jeans.

When you reach the gate, you can relax in the knowledge that you'll be the first person to board the plane. Gone are the days of stuffing a throw pillow under your shirt to fool dimwitted gate agents into letting you on first. Once aboard the plane simply hand your carry-on to the next passenger to stow in the overhead compartment. Even if she's ninety years old and wheeling oxygen behind her, she has to help you because guess what? You're pregnant, bitch!

NAMES

Naming your child is one of the most exciting things you will ever do. One day the commissioner of Major League Baseball might say his name when inducting him into the Hall of Fame, a Supreme Court Justice might announce her name when she's inaugurated as president, or countless chicks might cry out his name in ecstasy as he delivers the goods.

Naming your child is also one of the most terrifying things you will ever do. Screw up now and your child could spend the entirety of junior high crammed inside his locker because you thought the name Gayden was, like, *sooooo* cute. Focusing on a trendy name might also cause professional embarrassment for your child down the line. Nobody wants a lawyer named Cody or a doctor named Brooklyn . . . unless of course you're filming a porno.

And don't think you can just squeeze your cutesy little name into the middle either. Just imagine how mortified your son would be if, after killing and eating seventeen male prostitutes, everyone in the world finds out his middle name is Ashton.

After you've compiled a list of your favorite names you can test each one through the following rubric. If it passes all the criteria then you'll know it's a safe name for your child.

NAME STRESS TEST

- Does the name rhyme with any part of the human anatomy?

- Are you simply pirating the last name of a nineteenth-century American president?

- If so, can you name one act he accomplished while in office? (Other than lots and lots of sex, I'm assuming . . .)

- Memorize the following line, then close your eyes and say it out loud in a gravelly voice: "Gentleman, welcome to the stage . . . (CHOSEN NAME)!" If you find yourself reaching into your wallet for singles then it may not be the ideal name.

- Does the name seem like a name that might later be ascribed to a giant, anthropomorphic, extinct animal that despite its unquestioned zoological position as a carnivorous apex predator is painted purple and forced to teach children the value of sharing?

- Could your child ever join the likes of Blaze, Ice, Laser, and Turbo on *American Gladiators* and *not* have to change his or her name? 'Cause if so, that would be pretty friggin' awesome . . .

- Does it sound good before the world's greatest middle name: Waitforit?

GENDER

In the not-so-distant past you wouldn't know your baby's gender until it popped out and the doctor ceremoniously announced whether or not it had a dong. These days, thanks to science, you can learn your child's gender as early as eighteen weeks into the pregnancy.

Your doctor will perform an ultrasound and casually ask if you're interested in the sex. Try not to giggle—in this instance she's more than likely referring to "gender" and not "hot boning." Whether or not you want to know your child's gender is a personal question with no right or wrong answer. In fact, many parents are still unsure years and years later . . . Just ask Mr. and Mrs. Bieber.

If you do decide to look at the ultrasound, don't be discouraged—your child's penis or breasts aren't fully developed yet.

BARNEY'S "TIP"

If your partner asks whether you want a boy or a girl, the correct answer is "I'd be ecstatic with either." Lying and saying you want a girl could come back to bite you in the ass.

DID YOU KNOW?

Ultrasound technology was first developed in Austria in the late 1930s. Two nerdlinger scientists, having never seen a naked woman, built a complicated apparatus to fire concentrated sound waves through the wall into the lady scientists' locker room. It proved to be far more successful than their previous device—a portrait of composer Franz Schubert with the eyes cut out. True story.

UNCLE BARNEY'S ALPHABET BOOK

 is for AWESOME, which is what you'll always be.

 is for BOOBS, with a cup size larger than C.

 is for COCKTAIL, way cooler than a beer.

 is for *DIE HARD*, watch it twice a year.

is for EASY, the kind of chicks you'll claim.

 is for FRIENDS, who hopefully aren't this lame.

 is for GAMBLING, life's greatest joy.

 is for HORSESHOE, an underrated sex toy.

is for INDIANA JONES, minus *Kingdom of the Crystal Skull.*

 is for JOURNEY and JANE'S ADDICTION, but not for JETHRO TULL.

 is for KARATE, more awesome than kung fu.

 is for LEGENDARY, what your parents think of you.

is for ME, the best person in the world.

 is for NIPPLES, be they droopy, pointy, or curled.

 is for ONE NIGHT, how long a relationship should last.

 is for PORN, which you'll use to "rig your mast."

 is for QUARTERBACK, the position to play or bang.

 is for RED WINE, when a chick comes over to "hang."

 is for SUIT, the uniform for Bros.

 is for TUBE TOP, the uniform for hos.

is for USA! USA! USA!

 is for VAJAYJAY! VAJAYJAY! VAJAYJAY!

 is for WET T-SHIRT, two highlights of spring break.

 is for X-RAY, how you'll know they're fake.

 is for YOUTH, defined as under thirty.

 is for ZIPPER, it can chafe when you're getting dirty.

MULTIPLES

here is no more fear-inducing sentence in the English language than "You're having twins!" It means you'll need twice as many diapers, twice as many cribs, and twice as many nipples. But what exactly are twins?

Twins are identical copies of the same person and therefore share the exact same thoughts, personality, and wardrobe. While some twins can be hot (the Doublemint babes) and some twins can be creepy (the girls from *The Shining*), all twins are annoying. Can you imagine having to deal with two identical versions of the same thing all the time? Can you imagine having to deal with two identical versions of the same thing all the time?

To make matters worse, if you have female twins you'll have to constantly be on your guard: there are men out there who will make it their life's mission to have sex with them. Oh, also, if you have twin chicks and think they'll be cute in eighteen years, *dibs*!

As bad as it would be to have twins, imagine if you were diagnosed with triplets, quadruplets, or even quintuplets? According to science, it's biologically possible. The good news is if your triplets are even halfway attractive, then they're pretty much guaranteed a long career in the adult film industry . . . I'm talking like four to five hundred films over the course of two or even three years. The even better news is if you crank out quintuplets or more, you could be looking at a pretty lucrative reality show deal, provided you are totally screwed up and hot . . . well, TV hot anyway.

FAMOUS TWINS

Romulus and Remus

Mary Kate and Ashley Olsen

those fat motorcycle guys

Kirby Puckett

Xamot and Tomax

Dolly Parton

Arnold Schwarzenegger and Danny DeVito

Luke and Leia

those dudes from Harvard who thought they invented Facebook

Gary Busey and Nick Nolte

BIRTH PLAN

As you near your due date, it's important to create and review your "birth plan." This is the carefully prepared checklist of important last-second responsibilities that you will use as toilet tissue the second labor begins and you immediately crap your pants.

The first thing to decide is whether to give birth in a hospital or in your own home. While you might save a lot of money by having the birth in your home, be sure to ask yourself this question: "Will I ever be able to host Thanksgiving dinner in the same room I saw a vagina explode?"

The next thing to decide is whether to have a natural birth or a medicated birth. A natural childbirth means eschewing painkillers for the holistic experience of connecting with your child as he enters the world. A medicated childbirth means you're not a friggin' moron.

AM I REALLY GOING TO WANT PAIN MEDICATION?

By all accounts childbirth is the most pain you can experience without dying. That means having a child will hurt more than when Evel Knievel tried to jump the fountains at Caesar's Palace and shattered his pelvis, femur, hip, skull, ribs, wrists, and ankles before slipping into a twenty-nine-day coma. So, epidural? More like epi-*more*-al! Tell your ob-gyn to pretend the epidural is a heroin-filled syringe and your lower spine is Kurt Cobain's left arm circa 1993.

Since men don't get to experience childbirth from the driver's seat, I've created a chart that equates the agony of labor with some common, everyday aches and pains.

CHILDBIRTH PAIN CONVERTER

LABOR PAIN	MALE EQUIVALENT
Stretching of the birth canal	Losing an over/under because some jackass safety needlessly runs an interception ninety-nine yards to the house instead of just taking a knee to ice the game
Contractions	Mocking the employee at a home improvement store for offering a safety tutorial on power tools, then going home and promptly sawing off half your thumb
Bowels crushed by baby's head	The morning after three dozen spicy Buffalo wings and a pitcher and a half of hefeweizen
Cervical pressure	Blue balls
Vaginal laceration	The only woman who could make you happy, the only woman you've ever truly loved choosing another man over you. Umm . . . I mean taking a foul ball in the nuts! Youch, right? (Forget about that first thing, that was just a joke.)

PART III

EARLY CHILDHOOD

Okay, so the doctor yanked a baby out of you, cut the cord, and handed it back to you. Now what? The most important thing you can do is not flinch at the sight of your newborn. While doting grandparents and well-meaning friends will say your child is "beautiful" or "looks like an angel," the reality is he'll look more like a cross between a Mexican hairless terrier and former NBA player Sam Cassell.

Remain calm and remember that this awkward phase won't last. If for some reason it does, I suppose it's never too early to start a steady regimen of plastic surgery.

In this next section we will discuss the unique responsibilities that come with owning and operating a child in its first year. You'll find that caring for an infant can be as intense as caring for a good pair of leather shoes, though it's unlikely it will ever get you laid as much.

CIRCUMCISION

I f you have a boy, the first thing you'll need to get a grip on is his penis. That didn't come out right, but what I'm trying to say is that you'll need to make a circumcision decision, or "circumcision." That didn't come out right, either.

Whether or not to surgically remove the foreskin from your baby's wang is a surprisingly contentious issue. Aside from any religious or cultural considerations there's also a spirited debate raging in the medical community. Some believe that excess foreskin increases the chance of infection and disease, while others believe there are no significant benefits to chopping up your newborn son's wiener.

Then there's the issue of sexual pleasure. Studies have shown that an intact foreskin may increase sexual pleasure, while other studies have shown that taking a scalpel to your child's johnson may in fact decrease his pleasure.

To get a better sense of the infant perspective on circumcision, I commissioned a poll of 2,500 newborn males.

CIRCUMCISION PIE CHART

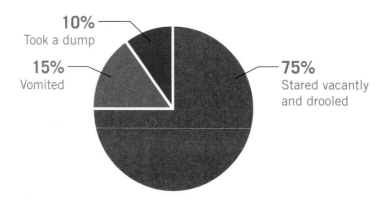

10%
Took a dump

15%
Vomited

75%
Stared vacantly
and drooled

THE FOX AND THE BRO

A foxy chick once saw a Bro enter a bar carrying a fat wad of cash in his hand. The fox thought to herself, "Even though I've never had a real job and don't possess nor have ever possessed a single employable skill, I deserve that cash, for I am a hot piece of ass." The fox approached the Bro and said, "Hello there, tall, dark, and handsome." The Bro's ears and other body parts perked up at her words. She continued, "Wow, you've got a couple of catcher's mitts for hands. I *looooove* big hands, because you know what that means . . ." "I sure do." The Bro knowingly winked. "It's really hard to text or open a bottle of aspirin." Exasperated with his idiocy, the fox tried again: "I mean, I wonder what your big hands would feel like upon my shockingly real boobs?" At this, the Bro reached his hands toward her rack like an elderly man trying to adjust the water temperature in a bath and promptly dropped the wad of cash on the floor. The fox swooped up the money and scampered out of the bar.

Never trust a hottie who talks to you first.

CHILD CARE

At some point you're going to need to leave your child. Whether you come back or not is up to you, but in the meantime you need someone to look after the baby. While a meddling parent or basket-case friend is a natural choice, a more permanent nanny may be the most flexible option . . . if you know what I mean. Wink!

There are many options available when hiring a nanny, which is fortunate because you should be highly selective. This person is going to be around your child and your home all the time, so you want someone who is timely, responsible, and just dirty enough to show a little thong.

As you conduct your search for the perfect nanny, don't be afraid to think globally. Importing a foreign national can be a fiscally savvy move because you can leverage her work visa and legal status for a much lower pay rate. Plus, with their broken English and open-mindedness toward nudity, many foreign women are major boner makers.

As you screen potential nannies, you'll need to look a little deeper than simply down her shirt. Here are some sample questions to ask as you conduct your nanny interviews.*

1. Would you ever hit or spank my child?

2. Would you ever hit or spank me?

3. My wife and I have a "secret open relationship." Are you familiar with that term?

4. Are you open to wearing a uniform of my design?

* Dibs on trying to sell *Nanny Interviews* to Cinemax.

5. Are you willing to sign release forms regarding the use of hidden "nanny cams"?

6. Would you be willing to help out with the occasional household chore like taking out the trash, walking the dog, or watering the T-shirts?

7. Show me, on your own body, how you would treat a diaper rash.

8. Our child has an active imagination. This may sound silly, but can you pretend you're a tiger stalking her prey? And might I remind you it's sweltering in the jungle . . .

HOW TO HANDLE THE BABY

Many of you are understandably nervous about holding your brand-new baby. If you do it wrong you could drop her. On the other hand you can't just stuff her in a backpack all day—that would be fashion suicide.

Here are a few safe and popular techniques for holding your baby while still looking bad-ass.

The Gunslinger

The Heisman

The Wayward Cub

The Michael Jordan

The World-Record Fish

BRO MACDONALD

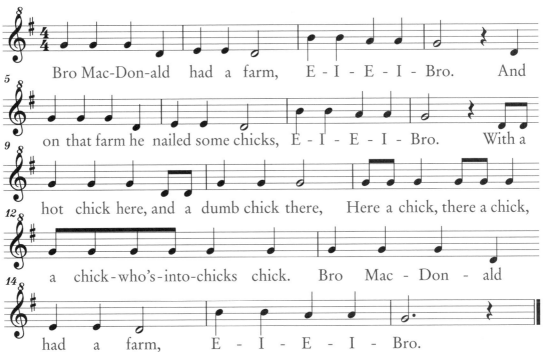

Bro MacDonald had a farm, E–I–E–I–Bro.
And on that farm he had some booze, E–I–E–I–Bro.
With a single malt here, and an añejo flight there,
Here a shot, there a chug, a cosmo for a lady's mug.
Bro MacDonald had a farm, E–I–E–I–Bro.

Bro MacDonald had a farm, E–I–E–I–Bro.
And on that farm he grew some weed, E–I–E–I–Bro.
With a puff-puff here, and a toke-toke there,
Crap, the cops! Grab the crops, and head out for the mountaintops!
Bro MacDonald had a farm, E–I–E–I–Bro.

Bro MacDonald had a farm, E–I–E–I–Bro.
And on that farm he wore a suit, E–I–E–I–Bro.
With a three-piece here, and a pinstripe there,
Here a tux, there a gray, a zoot suit for the NBA.
Bro MacDonald had a farm, E–I–E–I–Bro.

Bro MacDonald had a farm, E–I–E–I–Bro.
And on that farm he gambled on sports, E–I–E–I–Bro.
With a point spread here, and a parlay there,
Here a horse, there a dog, once a Laotian racing frog.
Bro MacDonald had a farm, E–I–E–I–Bro.

DIAPERS

hen it comes to diapers, you have two choices: cloth or disposable.

- Cloth diapers are more affordable, better for the environment, and drastically reduce diaper rash.
- Disposable diapers are what you will use.

Unfortunately, technology has not yet developed a self-immolating diaper, so you'll be forced to personally remove and dump out your child's dump-out. Worse, because infants are stupid and don't know how to speak, the only way to tell if they're feeling ill is by regularly inspecting their bowel movements, or as they're referred to in the pediatric vernacular, "caca."

The following illustrations help interpret some common messages your child will express to you through her doodie.

DID YOU KNOW?

The average baby will annihilate approximately 3,000 diapers in his first year. To put that in perspective, the entire cast of *The Golden Girls* only destroyed half that number in over seven years on the air.

"I'm hungry."

"How does this diaper make *you* feel?"

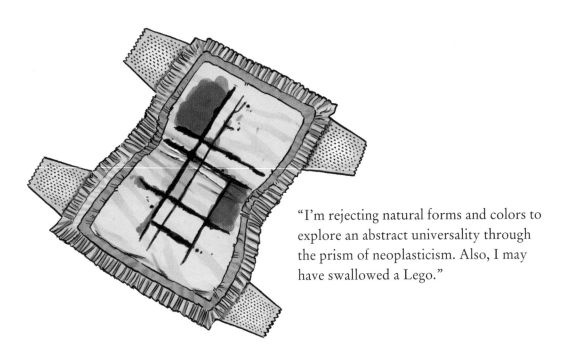

"I'm rejecting natural forms and colors to explore an abstract universality through the prism of neoplasticism. Also, I may have swallowed a Lego."

"Stare at this diaper. Do you see a vase, two faces, or me erupting like a urine geyser all over the carpet because you're busy staring at my stinky diaper?"

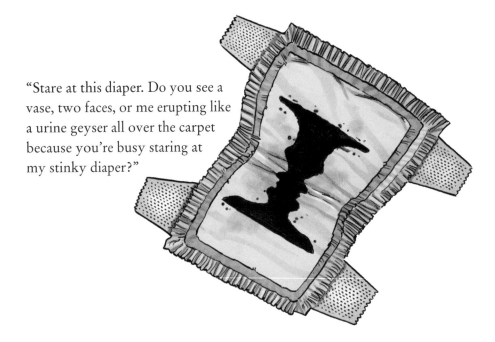

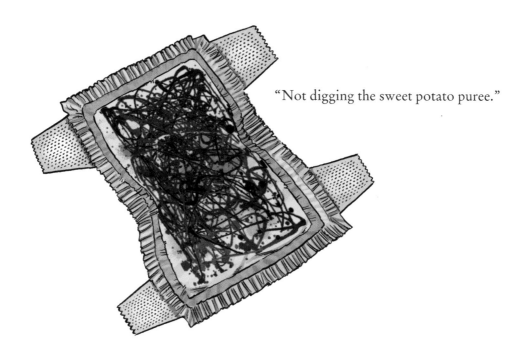

"Not digging the sweet potato puree."

"Just a normal poop.
No message here."

BIRTH ANNOUNCEMENT

fter you've given birth, you'll need a clever way to remind friends and family that it's time to buy you more crap for the baby. That's what birth announcements are for.

Most announcements include a picture, but since it's impossible to get a baby to stop puking or spraying diarrhea long enough to actually take a photograph, almost everyone uses the following, rights-free baby picture:

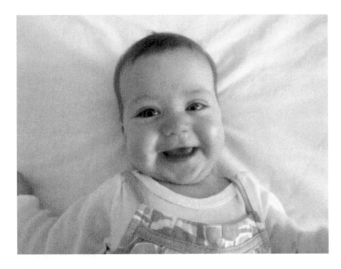

If you're worried that the baby doesn't look anything like yours, relax. To everyone but you, all babies look identical.

The actual write-up of your birth announcement is pretty straightforward, so to liven things up, why not try doing it Bro Libs style? Simply fill in the prompts, then match your answers to the text below, and you've got your baby announcement!

_____ and _____
　　　　Your name　　　　　　　　　　　　　　　Partner's name

are overcome with _____
　　　　　　　　　　　　　Strong emotion

at the arrival of our _____ ,
　　　　　　　　　　　　　　　Son or daughter

_____ _Waitforit_ _____ .
　　　　Baby's first name　　　　　　　　　　　　　　　Baby's last name

_____ _was born on_ _____ _____ , _____ ,
　　He or she　　　　　　　　　Birth month　　Birth day of　　　Birth year
　　　　　　　　　　　　　　　　　　　　　　　　　month

which means _____ _and I were_
　　　　　　　　　　　Partner's nickname

smacking _____ _sometime around mid -_
　　　　　　　　Part of the anatomy, plural

_____ . _Little_ _____ _tipped_
　Birth month + three months　　　　　　　Worst plausible nickname for your baby

the scales at _____ _pounds_ _____ _ounces._
　　　　　　　How many pairs of　　　　　　Age you sexually "awoke"
　　　　　　　shoes you own

Gifts aren't necessary but don't be a friggin' _____ .
　　　　　　　　　　　　　　　　　　　　　　　Barnyard animal

WARDROBE

Let's be honest—many of you only got pregnant and suffered through the pain of childbirth so you'd come out of it with a willing or at least defenseless live doll. You finally have a living, breathing creature that won't snarl and snap when you cram her into various cute outfits.

Well, I hate to burst your bubble, but that's totally lame . . . no matter how devastatingly cute or adorable they are when you dress them up to look like chubby little adults . . . like when you put a baby in a tiny baseball uniform complete with an itty-bitty baseball cap and everything and you call him your little slugger and you just want to squeeze him and squeeze him and squeeze him! *Totally* lame.

Anyway, so you won't be tempted to play dress up with your child, below are some fun cutout outfits for you to mix and match.

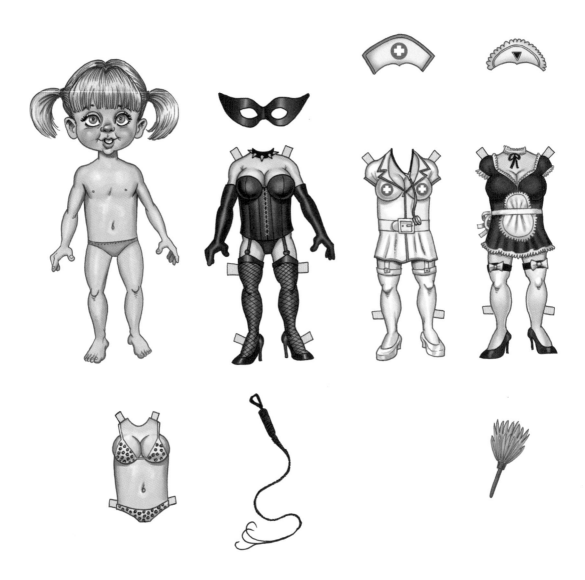

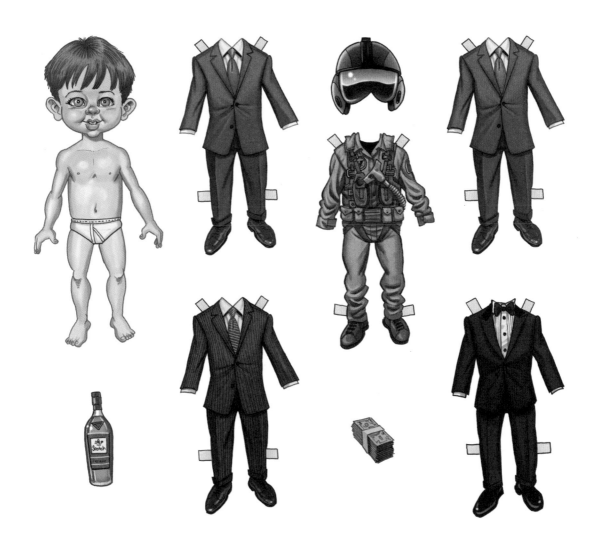

BREASTFEEDING

One of the more fascinating discoveries I made while conducting research for this book is that boobies are not just for dudes. Early speculation was that a woman's jugs swelled during pregnancy to help offset her ballooning gut, but apparently there's evidence to suggest that infants can actually draw milk when they motorboat their mommies' milk bags . . . oh duh, milk bags! I just got that!

Since letting your baby go to town on your melons is a healthy and affordable way to feed your child, you'll want to do everything possible to ensure it's done in a safe and socially acceptable fashion. Here are a few helpful breastfeeding tips.

- There are no laws against breastfeeding in public provided you're hot, in shape, and your baby is small enough that he won't obstruct everyone's view.
- Have your nonpregnant friends show their solidarity by asking them to occasionally flash the girls when out at the bar, on the JumboTron at a sporting event, or up against the window when they drive to work.
- Studies have shown that your breast milk can easily curdle if not consistently stirred. Ask your colleagues and even well-dressed strangers to fondle your headlamps to help keep that milk a-flowing!
- Babies are very sensitive and often develop rashes when exposed to various fabrics. For this reason try to go topless as much as possible.
- It's not uncommon for your nipples to dry and crack with your baby constantly chomping at your knockers like a starved piglet suckling a sow. A soothing balm like nipple butter can ease the pain when slowly applied in front of a streaming web camera.

THE TORTAS AND THE HAIR

There once was a Bro who lived down the street from a taco stand. He ate there so often, he had his own stool, could recite their menu blindfolded, and had even developed a confusing, flirtatious relationship with the seventy-year-old Mexican woman who sat out front and barked your order back into the kitchen. One day, after coming across a jaw-droppingly good Groupon, he decided to bring his Bros along. He recommended the machaca torta—a sandwich filled with dried, spicy beef. When the food arrived, the Bros absolutely crushed their tortas, for they were as delicious as promised. But just when they were going to leave and make preparations for an impromptu beer pong tournament, one of the Bros looked at his plate and saw a long, curly hair, forever ruining the taco stand for his Bro . . . and countless others after he posted a profanity-laden review on Yelp.

Never look at the food in your favorite Mexican restaurant.

BATH TIME!

his area makes me uncomfortable. You're on your own. Sorry.

GOLDISLUT AND THE THREE BROS

Once upon a time there were three Bros: Barney Bro, Marshall Bro, and Ted Bro. They were going out later for what would no doubt be another legendary night and decided to go pound some shots at the bar to get properly psyched.

Just then Goldislut, a blond hottie who lived upstairs, wandered into their pad, looking to borrow some sugar, if you know what I mean. She decided to sit down and wait for the Bros to get back. Barney's chair was too hard (what up!), Ted's chair was too soft, and Marshall's chair was okay I guess, though it leans awkwardly to the left and he should really get that checked out.

Soon Goldislut grew tired of waiting and went into the bedroom to lie down. Marshall's bed was too dirty, Ted's bed was too rigid from inactivity, but Barney's bed was just right, despite being so big—Goldislut liked it that way.

When the three Bros came home, they found their lair a mess. Marshall Bro said, "Someone's been sitting in my chair!" Barney Bro said, "Someone's been sitting in *my* chair!" And Ted Bro said, "At least something of mine is getting sat on."

They went into the bedroom and saw Goldislut asleep in Barney's bed. When she awoke, she winked sexily at Barney Bro but was understandably frightened by Ted Bro and Marshall Bro. Barney Bro kicked them out and gave Goldislut some sugar. Then he had sex with her.

The End

GETTING JACKED

Until your child can walk on his own, you'll be forced to carry him around in your arms since many cultures frown upon dragging a baby behind you on a tow rope. It can be quite the workout since it's just like carrying a 25 pound dumbbell everywhere you go . . . if the dumbbell squirmed, drooled, and frequently crapped all over itself. The good news is you'll quickly start to notice some dramatic muscle growth: your biceps will bulge out faster than when Popeye chugs a can of spinach, your triceps will harden faster than when Bruce Banner gets angry and hulks out, and your forearms will tone faster than when a fourteen-year-old hits puberty and starts cranking his deal like it's a stubborn can of spray paint.

STROLLER

One of the most important and exciting acquisitions you will make is the baby stroller. You don't want to feel like a prisoner in your own home, and a stroller affords you the freedom to go outside and interact with the world. Without it your kid would have to crawl outside on a leash, and that's just crazy—it would take forever to get anywhere.

Having a reliable and easy mode of transport for your child is important for several reasons:

1. FRESH AIR.

   Your baby churns out poop like a malfunctioning cement mixer. You're going to want to air him out every few hours.

2. CHICKS.

   Unless you happen to be Middle East royalty, women will not be delivered to your doorstep.

3. BARS.

   People will stare if you're trying to juggle your child and an expensive single malt. With a stroller you can use both hands to cradle your drink.

When choosing a stroller, it's easy to get confused with all the options. What color do I want? Do I want a jogging stroller? Is the collapsible model safe for my child? Forget all that nonsense. All you need is one that fits through the door of your local gentlemen's club. You're better served buying the cheapest one you can find and then customizing it on your own to turn your stroller into a "broller."

THE BROLLER

Noise-canceling handlebars

Boob cam

Diaper incinerator

Boob Cam

When you're out and about, countless women will lean into the stroller to coo over your bundle of joy. The 3–D equipped camera sewn into the hood will allow you to coo over *their* bundles of joy.

Noise-Canceling Handlebars

You're likely well aware that babies are terrific at crying, coughing, burping, and other obnoxiously loud disturbances. Amplified sound waves aimed directly at your head generate a sonic interference that silences your child and eliminates other ambient noise pollution like car horns, gunshots, chatty foreigners, and your baby mama blabbering on about her "near paralyzing postpartum depression" or some other nonsense like that. Women ... am I right, fellas?!

Diaper Incinerator

No more icky diaper disposals while you're out on the go. Simply chuck a freshly soiled diaper or spit-up-laden onesie into the burn barrel, where a furnace continuously fires at a crisp 1,300 degrees Fahrenheit, safely converting the waste into harmless methane, nitrogen, assorted heavy metal particulate, and sulfur dioxide emissions.

LICENSE TO CHILL: THINGS YOUR BABY CAN HELP YOU GET AWAY WITH

**J**ust like your pregnancy, your child's infancy is a terrific time to take advantage of others. Here are a few things you can capitalize on now that you've got a kid.

- **DUMP YOUR CRAPPY FRIENDS.** Requests to go antiquing or to check out that new brunch place with your partner's loathsome friends are easily defeated with a curt "Sorry. New baby."
- **TAKE LONG-ASS BREAKS.** Nobody really knows or wants to know how long it takes to breastfeed or change a diaper. Use this ignorance to your advantage at work by hitting up a matinee during your lunch break or by squeezing in a solid session of Modern Warfare 3 when you disappear into your office to "pump."
- **ESCAPE LAME FAMILY FUNCTIONS.** There's nothing worse than visiting with family, and your new arrival means they will be even more persistent and clingy and difficult to kick to the curb . . . unless, of course, you inform them that baby has a stomach bug. If they say, "We don't smell anything," there's always the nuclear option of deucing your own pants. Gross? Perhaps, but some of those Thanksgivings will be endless enough to make you at least consider it.
- **PACK ON POUNDS.** When you carry your baby, it's very difficult to discern where your figure ends and the baby begins. Now's a great time to just dig in and pork out.

- **MOVE TO THE FRONT OF THE LINE.** Since nobody wants to deal with a screaming baby, people will move aside to let you through. If you find yourself at the end of a long line and your baby isn't crying, a gentle pinch should kick-start the old waterworks. If it doesn't, you can always try some amateur ventriloquism and mimic the cry yourself.
- **FART IN PUBLIC.** Babies permanently reek of dried urine, diarrhea, and despair. This is your chance to cut one without regard for the innocent bystanders around you. Even if you let one rip and it blasts out like a foghorn, people will just assume your baby vomited . . . which he probably did.

UNCLE BARNEY'S TIP (HEH)

Now is a great time for you to finally get that breast augmentation you've always secretly coveted. Soon your hooters will shrink down to their normal size, so if you "up the cup" now, people are less likely to remember your tired, old, sad boobs.

FORMULA

While there's no set time to stop breastfeeding, most mothers decide to call it quits when they can successfully sand and refinish a hardwood floor using only a can of polyurethane and their ravaged nipples. Most likely, you will then feed your child formula—a liquid or powder-based milk supplement specifically designed for infants. It will run you, on average, about eighty-three dollars a six-pack, though savvy shoppers can usually find deals on recently expired bottles.

But rather than simply dump formula down your baby's throat, why not have a little fun with it and introduce her to the wonderful world of mixed drinks? Below is a menu of some popular formula cocktails. For added flair I recommend serving each with a lemon rind garnish and festive umbrella-shaped pacifier.

BABY'S FIRST COCKTAIL

DRINK	MIXOLOGY
Red Bull and Milk	½ whey-based cow milk formula
	½ caffeine-infused energy syrup
Spit and Colic	½ tonic water
	½ lime juice
Sleeptini	¾ soy-based formula
	¼ pureed olive
	1 crushed Ambien
Burpy Mary	¼ tomato juice
	¼ Tabasco sauce
	½ soda water
Irish Diaper Bomb	½ root beer
	¼ vanilla-flavored soy formula
	¼ Jameson Irish Whiskey

CAUTION!

For Fellas Only: When feeding your child, you will clean countless bottles and nipples. Avoid making comments comparing the various nipple shapes and sizes to real ones you saw in the field back in your glory days of being single. Yes, even if you once saw some in the size, shape, and color of a sombrero, a witch's hat, or rarest of them all, an airport windsock.

SLEEP

As a new parent the one thing you will miss more than financial stability, weekends, and pleasurable sex is sleep. Your infant is programmed to awaken with loud shrieks at the precise moment you drift into slumber. This is done to annoy you so much that eighteen years from now you won't blink twice before kicking his ass to the curb.

Fortunately I have extensive experience in lulling humans to sleep. Why? Because it's far easier to sneak out on someone you've just had sex with if they're asleep.

Here are some effective sleep strategies to employ with your child.

- **CRAPPY MOVIE**—Have your baby watch a slow and aimless feature film. I recommend *The English Patient*, *No Country for Old Men*, or anything directed by Paul Thomas Anderson.

- **STUFFED TURKEY**—You know how sleepy you get between football and pie on Thanksgiving? Same idea here. Simply feed your child a regular dinner of turkey, stuffing, cranberry sauce, deviled eggs, green bean casserole, and candied yams and he'll be asleep in no time.

- **TED**—Borrow my friend Ted and have him talk to your child about architecture or this great girl he just met who "could be the one!"

- **EXERCISE**—Put your child on an elliptical or treadmill for forty-five minutes to an hour. That oughta tucker the little bastard out.

■ **GET UNPSYCHED MIX** — Create a playlist of soft songs to lull your child to sleep. Here's a sample mix:

"Hurt" — Trent Reznor

"Brick" — Ben Folds Five

"Eleanor Rigby" — the Beatles

"Mad World" — *Donnie Darko* soundtrack

"I Hate Myself and Want to Die" — Nirvana

"Nothing Compares 2 U" — Sinead O'Connor

"How to Disappear Completely" — Radiohead

"Suicide Is Painless" — Theme from *M*A*S*H*

"Everybody Hurts" — R.E.M.

"Sounds of Silence" — Simon and Garfunkel

CRYING STRATEGIES

One of the biggest frustrations of early parenthood is the seemingly never-ending crying. Try as you may, nothing will stop the incessant sniffling, bone-rattling wailing, or soul-crushing bawling. To make matters worse, your baby is going to cry an awful lot too.

Honestly, you probably wouldn't give a crap if your kid *ever* slept at night if he would just shut the hell up, but he will erupt at even the slightest disturbance: a small change in temperature, a slightly damp diaper, a spirited yet classy key party with your kinky suburban neighbors.

If it seems like your child is crying inconsolably for more than three hours a day, he might have "colic"—a condition that causes extended periods of whining, moaning, and babbling for no discernible reason. I'm intimately familiar with this terrible affliction because my best friend Ted suffers from it.

Since excessive crying is so disruptive, many so-called experts have developed strategies to treat it. The most popular include

- **THE FERBER METHOD**—Ignore your kid.
- **THE SEARS METHOD**—Smother your kid (with attention, not a pillow).
- **THE 5 S'S**—Swaddle, Stomach position, Shushing, Swinging, Sucking . . . also an excellent technique for a hot date.

I tried all these methods on Ted and none of them worked, though swaddling did soothe him for about an hour before he got fussy and started blubbering uncontrollably.

If you really want to stop your child from crying, I recommend the MMMMM System, as espoused in the world-renowned Stinson Method.

- MUSIC—Since babies are easily distracted and soothed by music, movement, and physical touch, try taking your child to a strip club.
- MIRROR—Wait until your baby falls asleep and then cry loudly in her ear until she eventually learns just how friggin' annoying it is.
- MAN TO MAN—Sit your child down and give a brief but forceful explanation of why crying is unacceptable. Repeat as necessary.
- MOVE—Leave your home and return when the crying has stopped.
- MEDS—Many over-the-counter and under-the-counter drugs can mellow one's harsh. Whether you take them yourself or administer them to your baby is up to you, but keep in mind he'll probably never appreciate how much you paid for them.

BABY CRY TRANSLATOR

CRY	HUMAN TRANSLATION
Waaaaah! Ahhhhhhhhh! Ah ah . . . Waaah!	"Mother, I should like to suckle upon your ta-tas."
Aaaaaah! Yuh yuh aaaaaaaaaaaaaaaaaah!	"Seriously! Boobs! Now!"
Hooooooooooooooo! Hooooooo! Ahhhhhh.	"Hey, bitches! Check my britches!"
Hoooooooooo! Haaaaaaaaaaaa!	"Check out my Al Pacino impression!"
Aaaaaaaaah! Aaaaaaaaaah! Waaaaaaaah!	"Excuse me, I'm having difficulty rolling over."
Wah! Wah! Wah! Wah! Wah! Wah! Wah!	*"I don't know what I'm shouting about either!!!"*
Waaaaaaaaaaaaaaaaaaaaaaaaaaaaaaaaaah!	"Remember that diaper rash you've been reading so much about? Might want to take a little peekski at the old buttocks."
Ooooooooh! Waaaaaaah! Aaaaaaaah!	"Come here! I want to vomit on you!"
Ooooooooh! Aaaaaaaah! Waaaaaaah!	"Come here! I want to pee on you!"
Waaaaaaaaaaah! Waaaaaaaaaaaah! Urp.	"Just turned my onesie into a twosie!"

LULLABY

A lullaby is a song you sing to soothe your baby to sleep. The most popular English-language lullaby is "Rock-a-bye Baby," which has some surprisingly disturbing lyrics:

> Rock-a-bye baby, on the treetop,
> When the wind blows, the cradle will rock
> When the bough breaks, the cradle will fall,
> And down will come baby, cradle and all.

How disturbing are those lyrics when you really think about them? *Totally* out of date, right?! Who's putting a baby in a tree? Here are some awesome, modernized reboots:

> Rock-a-bye-baby, on the car top,
> When the mom drives, the bottle will tip,
> When the wheel jerks, the cradle will sway,
> And out will come baby, on the freeway.

> Rock-a-bye baby, at the bus stop,
> When the mom blows, she scores her crack rock,
> When the pimp calls, you'd better not squeal,
> If he finds the baby, sh*t will get real.

> Rock-a-bye-baby, at the chop shop,
> When the torch fires, the Camry will strip,
> If the parts break, they'll still make some dough,
> By selling the baby, in Mexico.

PLAYPEN

One of the coolest purchases you will make is the playpen, which will be your kid's first bachelor pad. Your child will spend upwards of sixteen hours a day in his playpen while you're out hanging with your Bros, so you'll want to outfit it with the latest and greatest that technology has to offer.

Forty-Inch Plasma TV

I know forty inches sounds ridiculously small for a TV, but to your infant, that's the size of an entire wall! As an added bonus, this screen size ensures your child will be continuously exposed to high levels of ultraviolet radiation so she'll be rocking a healthy bronze complexion after only half an episode of *Bubble Guppies*.

Baby's First Hot Tub

You probably won't be able to fit an actual tub in the playpen, but a hot plate and a large saucepan can serve as a crafty and fun alternative for your little ball of joy.

Fifteenth-Century Samurai Sword

Great conversation piece.

Rare Fish Aquarium

Introduce your child to the wonderful world of marine biology with her very own collection of puffer fish, stingrays, moray eels, poisonous box jellyfish, sea snakes, and, space-permitting, a fifteen-foot man-eating tiger shark.

BRO, BRO, BRO YOUR BROAT

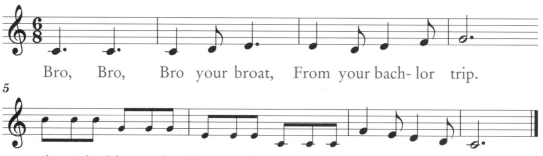

Bro, Bro, Bro your broat, From your bach-lor trip.

Blear-i-ly, blear-i-ly, blear-i-ly, blear-i-ly, why'd we bring a whip?

Bro, Bro, Bro your broat,
Gently toward the game.
Don't forget to bring your flask,
The price of beer's insane.

Bro, Bro, Bro your broat,
Gently to the bar.
Hit on sluts and do ten shots,
And vomit in the car.

Bro, Bro, Bro your broat,
Saw some girls strip bare.
Fairly, fairly, fairly sure
You left your Visa there.

Bro, Bro, Bro your broat,
Gently to the rave.
Barely, barely, barely clothed,
The chicks are all depraved.

Bro, Bro, Bro your broat,
Gently to the gym.
Do ten squats to wow a chick,
But dislocate a limb.

Bro, Bro, Bro your broat,
To the paintball yards.
Pretend that you're a war hero,
Who's blasted in the nards.

THE BRO WHO CRIED "HOT CHICKS"

There once lived a Bro who would text his Bros: "Hot chicks in the bar tonight!" When his Bros would arrive to wingman him, he would laugh at them for there were no hot chicks, just, like, a lot of dudes or something. The Bro did this a couple of times because he thought it was hysterical—and it kind of is—until one night he walked into the bar to discover a Hawaiian Tropic calendar shoot taking place. The Bro texted his Bros in terror: "Dudes, seriously need a wingman right now . . . hot-chick calendar shoot!" But this time his Bros paid no heed to his cry, nor did they leave their video game marathon to assist him. The Bro tried to score a bikini babe on his own, but with no wingman, he was torn to pieces by the entire flock.

There is no believing a Bro who lies about hot chicks,
even when he speaks the truth.

PART IV

TODDLERDOM

W hen your child finally reaches one year old, he will no longer be an infant; he will be a toddler. These next two to three years promise to be a magical time during which your own flesh and blood will learn to walk, speak whole sentences, and slowly discover that excrement belongs in a toilet and not smeared all over his face.

It's also a time when your child will begin interacting with other children on playgrounds, at birthday parties, and wherever else you'll drag your kid in the hopes of meeting other desperate single parents looking to score a quickie before returning to the drudgery of parenthood.

This is a formative time for your toddler, as he will first learn the social skills he'll need to rely on as an adult. That's why this is the perfect time to start teaching your little boy how to talk to girls or your little girl how to talk to girls about other girls behind their backs.

BIRTHDAY PARTIES

When your child turns one, you will be tempted to celebrate her first birthday with a party even though she'll have no idea what's going on, never remember it, and will likely vomit cupcake all over her brand-new top . . . Come to think of it, it won't be much different than her twenty-first birthday.

When planning your child's first birthday, be sure to invite everyone you know who has a kid even if you kinda hate them and their kid is already a giant turd. Why? Because you never know who will turn out rich and famous, and a photo of that kid at your kid's birthday could be worth a fortune when the U.S. Congress is finally overthrown by TMZ.

As you go over your guest list, you will be very tempted to invite your single friends and favorite childless couples. If you do, know that they will forever hate you for guilting them into attending such a stupid event and will likely never speak to you again. Whatever you decide, just make sure there's plenty of booze to go around.

Guess who finally made a #1 that didn't spray us in the face?

Join us as we celebrate our little douchebag's first birthday! Come keep an eye on the birthday boy while we attempt to make up for almost two years of forced sobriety in just under three hours. Clothing optional.

WHERE: **Dirty Jim's Liquor Store**

WHEN: **Saturday afternoon, at exactly the same time as the big playoff game . . . just like last year when the bastard was born.**

PRESCHOOL

Although your child won't attend preschool for another interminable year or two, it's never too early to start greasing palms at the best one. Studies have shown that the more exclusive the preschool your child attends, the better chance he has of making a fortune, marrying a swimsuit model, owning a vacation home in Vail, and ultimately shooting himself in the head when the SEC finally catches up with him . . . Don't you want to give your child that opportunity?

You've probably heard that the odds of getting accepted at your top local preschool are pretty low. The unfortunate truth is they are. Acceptance rates at the best preschools are often well under 10% once you subtract families that already have children in the school, parents who have donated lots of money, and eager mothers who've supplied enough "favors" that you could rename the admissions office the "emissions office."

Since you definitely want your child to attend a top-tier preschool, I strongly recommend one of the following options:

1. Give enough money to fund a new sports facility, science lab, or private jet.

2. Entrap the admissions director with a classy prostitute, take pictures of the encounter, then hand deliver them to the director in a manila envelope with your child's application enclosed.

3. Hire a little person actor to ace the interview. (If you want the very best, book Peter Dinklage. He'll probably demand an executive producer credit, but let's be honest: your child has a much better chance of getting greenlit by the preschool if Dinklage is attached.)

POTTY TRAINING

When you've grown tired of changing diapers, it's time to teach your kid how to use the toilet or, as the experts call it, the "potty." By all accounts this will not be an easy endeavor. Apparently your child will behave like using the can is the most frightening thing in the world, and this from someone who's never stepped foot in a gas station stall or airport crapper.

One of the greatest challenges of potty training is the sheer number of "transactions" your child goes through. A toddler can pee up to twenty times a day—that's as often as an incontinent senior citizen, a drunk frat guy, or your average chick. As far as poop goes, let's just say at times your child's rear end will resemble the soft-serve machine at a Dairy Queen.

With that kind of waste production, removing diapers from your kid probably seems about as intelligent as switching the safety off an assault rifle and handing it to a self-appointed border patrolman on Cinco de Mayo. To help protect your furniture, flooring, and household pets from damage when the crap literally hits the fan, I recommend putting newspapers down all over the house . . . provided they're still printing them.

GOODNIGHT
BRO

by Barney Stinson
Pictures by Tom Richmond

In the little Bro's room

There was a fancy globe bar

And an electric guitar

An Asian porn star.

And a massage chair on an endangered bear

And a rack of suits

And gravity boots

Goodnight Xbox

Goodnight insider stocks

Goodnight stars

Goodnight busty widow

Goodnight Bro

BABY STEPS

One of the great joys of parenthood is watching your child learn to crawl and walk. Why is it so enjoyable? Because with every tiny step you inch closer and closer to finally ditching that goofy-ass frontal baby carrier.

As your child becomes increasingly mobile, you'll need to become increasingly vigilant. The sad truth is that it doesn't take much for your little adventurer to find tragedy: look away for even a second and she could easily walk out the door, out onto the street, and into a discount clothing store.

Because of these fears some parents choose to walk their child on a leash, which they pretend isn't demeaning because it connects to a harness hidden inside a colorful, animal-themed backpack.

Of course if safety is your primary concern, then a leash simply won't cut it. For less than sixty dollars you can get yourself a ground stake, a good length of galvanized steel chain, and a choke collar to set up a toddler run in your backyard. If you've got a bigger budget, you can always spring for the more aesthetically pleasing electric fence. Note: If you have coyotes, bears, or other large predators in your area, you might consider arming your toddler with a high-powered handgun or crossbow.

TELEVISION

Parents have mixed feelings about television. Some worry about all the sex, language, and violence and prefer to expose their children to slightly more wholesome stories like those found in the Bible about genocide, beheadings, and a man being nailed to a piece of wood and left to die.

The truth is it's hard to know what programming is safe for your child. To help you make an informed decision on what to let your child watch, here are a few television shows and movies to keep an eye on.

SAFE FOR CHILDREN	WHY
South Park	Children *love* animation.
Kill Bill	Bolsters positive samurai values like honor, loyalty, and bloodthirsty vengeance.
Pet Sematary	Gives children hope that even when your pets die, they never really leave you.
The Godfather	Teaches the importance of family.
Die Hard	Umm . . . it's awesome?

UNSAFE FOR CHILDREN	WHY
Sesame Street	Promotes unhealthy puppet fetish and may turn children into furries.
Veggie Tales	Anthropomorphic vegetables frighten children away from eating actual vegetables.
The Texas Chainsaw Massacre	Could actually bore your child to death.
Hannah Montana	Might be uncomfortable for you to watch now that Miley Cyrus is finally older than eighteen.
Winnie the Pooh	Teaches children that bears are not ferocious wild animals but, rather, cuddly, stuttering diabetics.

COMPETITION

At some point your child will encounter her first competition, whether she's interested in dancing, athletics, or total dork-bomb exploits like math and science. Suddenly, you'll be surrounded by parents spouting new age garbage like, "Everyone gets to play," and "We're all winners no matter what the scoreboard says," and "Just because Jacob struck out looking with the tying run standing on third doesn't give you the right to spit at him . . . I mean for crying out loud, you're an adult!"

Like it or not, in the real world there are winners and losers, and the sooner your child learns that lesson, the better equipped she'll be to handle the challenges of life. That's why it's a good idea to have your child watch as you ensure victory by bribing the referees or judges. Many of them will be high school kids, so it won't cost much. Start by offering a six-pack of domestic beer and see where it goes from there.

Once the competition begins, you'll need to keep your own emotions in check. As hard as it is to watch your child compete, it's even harder to avoid acting like you normally would as a spectator. Here are some common pitfalls to avoid.

DON'T

Wear a replica of your child's jersey with the number 69—the humor will be wasted on most of the crowd.

Start a "You suck!" cheer aimed at your child's sucky teammate.

Open an impromptu sports book and take action on everything from point spreads to proposition bets like "first kid to break down crying."

Purchase a kegerator, a trailer-mounted barrel grill, and a forty-five-foot luxury motor coach so you can properly tailgate before every game.

Streak the field.

133

DISCIPLINE

When it comes to disciplining your child, there are many different approaches. Some parents choose to set clear rules and consistently and fairly enforce them, while other parents choose to be awesome.

No matter which philosophy you pursue, eventually your kid will do something that requires correction, be it touching the stovetop, punching the family dog, or finding Daddy's video collection that was carefully hidden in an old bowling bag at the back of the garage.

Now, obviously you can't spank your child—the practice is abusive, antiquated, and best left for grown adults in the bedroom—so what's the healthiest way to discipline your child? Try giving one of these techniques a spin.

Time-out . . . side	You've probably heard of a "time-out" before—making your child sit quietly in the corner for 10 minutes. That's far too comfortable. Studies have shown you get better results by making him sit quietly *outside* for 10 minutes. This strategy is particularly effective in the dead of winter.
Crappy TV	Force your child to watch an entire episode of *Grey's Anatomy*, *The View*, or anything featuring Chelsea Handler.
Waterboarding	If it works for the CIA, it should work for you.
Decreased bandwidth	Nothing will spark good behavior faster than sabotaging the Wi-Fi connection on your toddler's laptop or smartphone.
Cash	They say that money talks. In this case, money can shut the hell up for the last fifteen minutes of *Mad Men*.

WHERE THE WILD CHICKS ARE

STORY AND PICTURES BY BARNEY STINSON

TRAVEL

raveling with your toddler is a nightmare. When you leave home, you'll need to haul along all of your child's essentials, like food, wipes, toys, and veterinary-grade sedatives.

No matter how long your trip is, your child will likely get motion sickness, act cranky, and whine nonstop until you reach your destination. This is a huge problem because when you're out in public, you can't just slap a muzzle on him and earplug up like you do at home.

The good news is that if you're traveling in a car, you won't have to constantly monitor him since many states actually require you to imprison your child in a safety seat. Even if he manages to chew through the straps and start acting up, you can always drown out the chaos by lowering all the windows and cranking up some AC/DC. If things really get out of hand, there's always the trunk.

Unfortunately, if you're traveling anywhere by airplane, you're screwed. Rest assured that by the time the use of approved electronic devices has been permitted, everyone sitting within fifteen rows of your child will have already fantasized about gagging him with a drop-down oxygen mask. Sure, you can ease their pain by marching him up and down the aisle to torture others for a while or offering to buy them drinks when he decides to emulate an ambulance siren for forty minutes straight, but the sad reality is that no matter what you do, everyone will be silently rooting for a sudden and catastrophic loss of hydraulic pressure.

That's why I'm proposing Toddler Air—an airline exclusively for shrieking kids and their beleaguered parents. Once aboard one of our majestic aircraft you will instantly relax and fly guilt-free knowing that every child contributes equally to the deafening din of wails, the foul stench of soiled diapers, and the violent shuddering of kicked seatbacks. Sure, we may have a little trouble attracting a flight crew and may only fly in and out of Orlando, but with our significantly lighter payload we will save a buttload on jet fuel.

Alexander and the Awesome, Legendary, Epic, Very Kickass Day

BARNEY STINSON

Illustrated by TOM RICHMOND

I went to sleep wasted last night after a six-hour Scotch tasting but when I woke up there wasn't even the slightest hint of a hangover and the Norwegian lingerie model I picked up must have bought the sexviction story I fed her about limiting her exposure to my nuclear-powered penis because there was no hint of her either and I could tell it was going to be an awesome, legendary, epic, very kickass day.

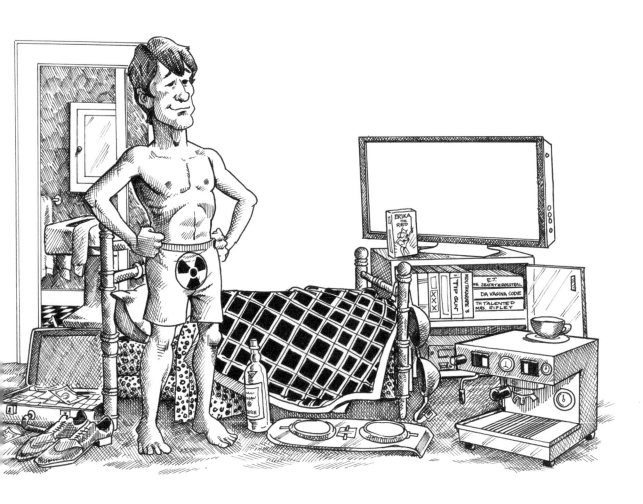

At work my boss promoted me yet again and this time I was given Mr. Schmidt's corner office and his racked-out secretary even though Mr. Schmidt has been at the company for thirty years and probably has a far better grasp of exactly what it is our company does and/or produces.

During my lunch break I found a $1,000 bill, watched a cab splash a puddle all over a hot chick in a white top, heard a couple get in a huge fight in their apartment, and saw a

pigeon dump out on some dude's head and I could tell it
was going to be an awesome, legendary, kickass day.

After work I went to the doctor and she told me I could eat whatever I want because I had 0% body fat and that my blood work and liver panel indicated my renal system was in fact quite robust and not "something we need to take a closer look at" and I could attend a Scotch tasting every day for the rest of my life and still live to be 120 years old with no visible signs of aging and that I was in the 99th percentile for penis length, which she realized when I needed her help collecting my urine sample. I could tell it was going to be an awesome, legendary, kickass day.

When I went to bed my guest let me use my expensive recording equipment and offered to do something she'd never done before and said she couldn't stay because she had to get back to her family but that I could go to her office for a free "physical" anytime I wanted.

It has been an awesome, legendary, kickass day.

COLLEGE

Attending college can provide your child with a number of life advantages. Statistically speaking he will earn twice as much money if he chooses to go to school rather than get high in your basement and play old-school Sega Genesis games. He will also get laid twice as much . . . even if all he does in college is get high and play old-school Sega Genesis games.

Unfortunately there's a hefty and ever-rising cover charge to get into the best colleges. At the time of this printing the average annual tuition at a private college is $35,000. After accounting for inflation, faculty pay raises, and ever-climbing student athlete salaries, the average annual tuition eighteen years from now will be $983,000, and that's not even including money for necessities like housing, textbooks, and Adderall.

Well-meaning parents, family members, and financial planners will encourage you to invest your precious money in a college savings account such as a 529 plan. This is an evil instrument that allows you to make tax-deferred contributions, annually deduct them from your state income tax returns, and make tax-free distributions for educational purposes when your child reaches the age of eighteen. There are far more lucrative things you can do with your money. Trust me, I work for a Wall Street bank.

The truth is you'll never be able to afford college through traditional savings. Sure, you can always try for a scholarship, but don't get your hopes up—those are traditionally reserved for students who get good grades, excel in sports, or have thirty-five minutes to fill out the application. What you'll need to do is somehow make a lot of money in a short amount of time. Studies have shown the best way to do that is to start an underground crime syndicate, work as a drug mule, or create your own "make money fast" program and sell it on late night television to other desperate idiots.

Ironically, one of the best ways to quickly make a ton of money is to start up your own college, offer every student a federally approved financial aid package to help defray the cost of tuition, and then charge exorbitant rates and hidden fees on the loan. It's one of the best scams going! And if you happen to open your school online, you won't even have to put on pants! Here's a quick profile of my own "nonprofit" accredited learning institution . . .

BARNEY STINSON UNIVERSITY

Location:	Cyberspace
Total Enrollment:	3–4 a night
Male/Female:	0/100
Endowment:	Blessed
Acceptance Rate:	12%
Acceptance Rate When I'm Drunk:	50%
Tuition:	$250/hr
Average Tests Scores:	600 Math, 550 Verbal, 800 Oral
Housing:	Guaranteed for the first 45 minutes but then you gotta go 'cause my parents are in town or something.
Strongest Programs:	Asian American Studies, Bedroom Theater, Bidness, Biochemistry, Hidden Cinema Arts, Horizontally Applied Physics, Prelaw, Premedicine, Prebanging, Radiation Oncology and Molecular Imaging, Silent Communications, Slutty Nursing, Women's Studies
Team Nickname:	The Fighting Barnacles

THE UGLY NERDLING

Once upon a time there lived a family with three daughters. The first daughter was hot and the second daughter had a body that could stop traffic, but the third daughter was an absolute train wreck from the waist up. She was bulbous and patchy and had a weird acne thing going on that unfortunately didn't do quite enough to distract you from her gigantic schnozzola.

Because of her repulsive appearance she was forced to focus on academics while at school, which only made her a bigger target . . . were that physically possible given her refrigerator-like dimensions. Everyone teased her and called her names like "Blimpy" and "Tubmo." One day even the principal called her "Porkerella" in front of the whole school when he accidentally left the intercom on after morning announcements.

She had no friends, and the only boys who showed any interest were simply using her to get to her smoking hot sisters. One day she came close to ending it all but failed to find a beam strong enough to support her, given that she weighed about the same as a fully loaded Toyota Rav4. Girl was fat.

Then one day she was given a high-paying job because she was so good at academics. She saved her money for five whole years, then had gastric lap band surgery, rhinoplasty, a brow lift, laser skin resurfacing, an experimental orthognathic procedure where surgeons were actually rearranged her facial bones with a series of controlled fractures, breast augmentation, and a double chinectomy.

Seventeen months later when the swelling had subsided and she was allowed to remove her bandages, she looked in the mirror and couldn't believe it. "Ffg mrrpkl essgty bt!" she said, her lips still numb from a last-minute collagen injection. She was so hot that everyone who looked at her popped an insta-boner . . . even chicks. Those mean boys who only wanted to bang her sisters now also wanted to bang her. She was so happy she almost burst . . . which, sadly, she did years later when the lap band finally buckled.

The End

JACK AND JILL

Jack and Jill went all the way
To end their first blind date.
Jack snuck home and failed to phone
Till Jill found out she's late.

LITTLE JACK HORNY

Little Jack Horny
While watching porn he
Dry humped an ottoman;
With all that he saw
He rubbed himself raw
And said, "I need to meet someone."

MARY HAD A LITTLE BANG

Mary had a little bang
Who she gave the old heave-ho.
But everywhere that Mary went
This dude was sure to go.

He followed her to work one day,
Which was against the law.
It made her colleagues point and say,
"I think he stole your bra."

She had to get a court order,
But still he lingered near.
He hid outside of her back door,
Till Mary would appear.

"What the F is your deal, bro?"
Did Mary shout and cry.
"Mother left me in Costco,"
The stalker did reply.

FIRST WORD

When your baby finally says her first word it will be a bittersweet moment, because once she can string together an entire sentence, she'll be ready to head off and face the world on her own. But knowing if she's said her first word can be a challenge given the number and variety of sounds constantly emanating from her area of operation. As a general rule it's unlikely her first word will be "blppppprrrrrt" and accompanied by the sudden smell of feces.

If you're like many parents, you've been secretly hoping her first word will be "Mama" or "Dada." Perhaps you've even got a fun little wager going with your partner. Perhaps you've even been coaching your child in private to say your name. Perhaps you've even caught your child saying the other name and threatened to withhold food until she says your name first so you can win that friggin' wager.

The truth of the matter is that you really don't want your kid's first word to be something lame and largely unintelligible like "Mama" or "Dada"—you want her to say something awesome, because then you know your kid's not going to be a dud.

BABY'S FIRST WORD TRANSLATOR

FIRST WORD	MEANING
"Awesome."	Your kid's gonna kick ass.
"Poop."	There's a cleanup in your future.
"Money."	Your child will lead a meaningful life.
"Threesome?"	You're raising a player.
"Boobies."	Either you've got a little horndog or he's just hungry.

CONCLUSION

Once you've sent your kid to school, your parenting duties are largely over. From now until the time she leaves the house for good, your role will shift from primary caretaker to that of a disinterested landlord who's occasionally forced to attend a birthday, teacher's meeting, or court date.

LOOKING DOWN THE ROAD

Looking down the road as parents, you're going to encounter a few landmark moments:

THE BIRDS AND THE BEES
Most kids learn about banging from their friends, but if your kid is a loner or a complete idiot, you might have to explain everything. Since this is likely to be an awkward conversation, it's best to sit him down when he's relatively calm, look him in the eye, and say, "Google it." Since many children are visual learners, you can always pop in a tame, early eighties porno and ask him afterwards if he has any questions. If he does, cross your fingers they're not about the plot.

DATING
Many parents wonder at what age their child can start dating. The answer is simple: "It depends on how hot she is." As a rule, if you find yourself fantasizing about one or more of your daughter's friends, then your daughter's probably old enough to date. Just be sure not to rush her into dating, since everyone develops at different speeds. Heck, my friend Ted is in his thirties and as far as I'm concerned hasn't had a real date yet.

DRIVING
Teaching your child to drive can be a frustrating, nerve-racking, and at times litigious experience. That's why it's safest to get him a fake ID, hotwire a car, and set him loose on the streets. That way if he gets into an accident and messes up the car, it won't negatively affect your insurance premiums.

If you can successfully navigate these waters, you'll be able to rest happy and proud, confident in the knowledge that even if your child never becomes president or gets married or contributes in any way to the local community, at the very least he's statistically unlikely to go nuts and open fire in a grocery store or public square. And really, isn't that all you can ask for as a parent?

TROUBLESHOOTING AND FAQS

What do I do if my child seems sick?

Dealing with a sick child is one of the more harrowing experiences you'll have as a parent. Given the amount and variety of fluids your child is likely to expel when sick, it's also one of the more nauseating experiences. The best thing to do if your child seems sick is to have him "walk it off." This tried-and-true therapeutic response has helped countless athletes overcome getting whacked in the nuts, and there is no more serious medical condition than that.

You should also resist the urge to immediately rush to the hospital. Hospitals are notorious for their cost, crappy food, and fluorescent lighting, which, let's face it, isn't exactly going to do wonders for your skin tone. More to the point, for all their monogrammed smocks, specialized license plates, and prescription pad privileges, you have to wonder about the quality of today's doctors, given the list of people who've been awarded a PhD.

- DR. NO—Famed James Bond villain who decided to base his multimillion-dollar aerospace enterprise in Jamaica . . . like he was starting up a marijuana co-op or an Olympic track and field school as opposed to a high-tech, nuclear-powered facility for applied astrophysics.
- DR. ROBERT BENTLEY—the governor of Alabama who tried to legally change his first name to "Dr." so it would appear that way on the ballot, foolishly assuming that would have any effect upon his largely illiterate electoral base.
- DOCTOR WHO—That weird British scientist guy with a legion of nerdy fans, which, ironically, is the only thing keeping me from checking out the show because I've actually heard good things. It's in my Netflix queue.

- **DR. DOOLITTLE** — A guy with the "ability" to speak with animals. When I was growing up, there was a man down the street who would sing entire operas to a trash can, but I don't recall anybody rushing to give that dude an advanced degree.
- **DOC BROWN** — How can the same man who cracked time travel by inventing the flux capacitor decide to install such cutting-edge technology in a 150 horsepower DeLorean? I'm confused: was Hill Valley Ford completely out of Mustangs that year or something?

My child seems way too attached to his "binkie." Should I be concerned?

Yes.

My dog is not getting along with our baby. What should I do?

If after a few months it seems like your pet is just not getting along with your child, you might be forced to make a difficult decision. On the one hand we're talking about a human life that you love like you've never loved anything before. On the other hand, your dog was there first, and even though he farts a lot and will eat the occasional turd, he's relatively cheap to own and never makes a sound louder than a whimper when he sleeps. Plus, he's reeled in far more chicks than that baby ever will. Yeah . . . keep the dog.

My wife hasn't had sex with me since the baby arrived. Should I try putting her breast pump on my wang?

No. Absolutely not. Please don't ask me how I know this.

It seems like now that my kid can finally talk, all she can say is, "Why?" Why is she doing that?

Great, now she's got *you* doing it. The incessant questions are one of the most annoying things about your kid, next to the drool, the inability to sleep more than three hours at a time, and the desire to watch the same animated movie no less than eighty-three times a day at the absolute maximum volume. Your best defense when asked "Why?" is to employ one of your child's greatest weapons—mimicry. The next time she asks, "Why?" just ask her, "Why?" in a high-pitched, mocking tone. After a few volleys back and forth she'll eventually get bored with you, give up, and return to the deafening adventures of a bombastic zebra or a stoned panda or whatever asexual character the repressed computer geeks in Silicon Valley decided would most appeal to every single four-year-old on the planet.

ABOUT THE AUTHORS

BARNEY STINSON is awesome. When he's not busy penning best-selling books or blowing up the blogosphere with www.barneysblog .com, Barney spends his precious time seducing buxom bimbos, collecting and consuming rare Scotches, posing as a backstage photographer at fashion shows, staging underground gladiatorial events, gardening, studding out one of his eighty-three Thoroughbred racehorses, working at a Wall Street bank, and making very brief appearances at charity events . . . like, long enough to get photographed but not so long that he'd be expected to write a check or know what the charity does.

MATT KUHN is a writer for the TV show *How I Met Your Mother.* In addition to producing "Barney's Blog" and drumming for Robin Sparkles, he has written eight episodes for the show featuring such special guest stars as Bryan Cranston, Jennifer Lopez, and "Weird Al" Yankovic . . . yes, *that* "Weird Al." This is his fourth book in collaboration with Barney Stinson after *The Bro Code*, *Bro on the Go*, and *The Playbook*. Matt makes his home in Los Angeles with his wife, Alecia, and their dog-turned-fashion-model, Maggie.

OWN

THE COMPLETE
SEASON
ON DVD
FALL 2012

7

includes awesome extras
exclusive to dvd!